# A Modern Greek Cookbook

'With respect to the culinary heritage of our land,
we create modern Greek food.'

# A Modern Greek Cookbook

**OPSO**

Andreas Labridis                    Nikos Roussos

MODERN GREEK FOOD

- 8 Introduction
- 14 The Greek Larder
- 32 Salads & Vegetables
- 50 Seafood
- 88 Meat
- 106 Barbecue
- 150 Greek Brunch
- 194 Baking
- 218 Pastry
- 260 Basic Recipes
- 278 Index
- 284 Acknowledgements

# Contents

# ANDREAS LABRIDIS

I love food … not only in the strict meaning of eating food but also everything around it. Food is the centrepiece of the happy moments in life, traditions, celebrations and seasonal festivities. Food brings people together.

But food is much more than that. It tells the story of a country's history, it carries traditions over from one generation to the next, and it makes people travel the length and breadth of this world to discover something new and to sample and enjoy different cuisines. In most countries, the food has evolved over time through a combination of hardship, migration, climate, landscape and the local produce from the land, rivers, lakes and sea. I am fascinated by the history of food and the way in which recipes vary not only from region to region but also by how many countries have essentially the same dish, albeit with small variations, and a story behind it and how it evolved.

My earliest memories are of enjoying being around food, whether it was helping in my mum's kitchen, watching my yiayia (grandmother) make halva, going to the local grocer with my dad or picking wild oregano and olives in the mountains of Halkidiki during the summer. I will never forget the time I went to collect honey from the beehives and was chased down the hill by what seemed – and felt – like hundreds of bees.

After graduating from high school in Greece, I decided to move to London and pursue a career in finance. I guess my way of thinking at the age of 17 gave priority to a lucrative career as opposed to the long hours and lower pay of working in a restaurant kitchen. However, 15 years ago I made a huge decision to change my path in life and take my first steps into the world of food and hospitality. My journey from the world of banking to London's lively culinary scene has been nothing short of extraordinary. Following my deep-rooted passion for food and a penchant for innovation with Greek flavours, I set out to create something truly unique, the first modern Greek restaurant in London. A restaurant that seamlessly blends the rich culinary traditions of Greece with contemporary techniques and flavours, while being true to my heart and my memories, bringing this new and innovative cuisine to London's West End.

In pursuing my dream of introducing modern Greek cuisine to London, I sought to challenge preconceived notions and to elevate the perception of Greek food beyond the traditional taverna fare. By adapting classic recipes using modern techniques, utilising locally sourced ingredients, and embracing global culinary influences, my aim was to offer an unforgettable dining experience that celebrates the essence of Greek hospitality and its culinary heritage.

Through dedication, creativity and a commitment to excellence, I am proud to have established a culinary destination that has garnered acclaim and captured the hearts of diners seeking a fresh perspective on Greek cuisine. This cookbook encompasses that journey. It is a tribute to the vibrant flavours, cultural richness and innovative spirit that define modern Greek food.

Through the recipes featured in this book, I invite you to join us on a gastronomic adventure showcasing the rich tapestry of Greek flavours, reimagined for the modern palate. Drawing inspiration from our upbringing in Greece and our extensive travels, we have curated a collection of recipes that celebrates the diversity and versatility of the modern Greek kitchen.

However, this cookbook is much more than just a collection of recipes; it's a testament to the transformative power of following your passion and pursuing your dreams. It's a celebration of the resilience, creativity and entrepreneurial spirit that drive individuals to forge their own paths and make their mark in the world. So, whether you're a seasoned home cook looking to expand your horizons or a curious food lover eager to explore the flavours of Greece, I invite you to join us on this culinary journey. Together, let's discover the magic of modern Greek cuisine and celebrate the joy of cooking, eating and sharing good food with those we hold dear.

Welcome to a culinary journey like no other, a celebration of modern Greek flavours, reimagined for a new generation of food enthusiasts.

**ANDREAS**

# NIKOS ROUSSOS

As I reflect on my culinary journey, which has taken me from the busy streets of Manhattan to the vibrant dining scene of London, I am full of gratitude for the incredible experiences, challenges and accomplishments that have shaped my career as a chef. With over two decades of dedication to the craft of cooking and a relentless pursuit of innovation and bold flavours, I am honoured to present my first cookbook, a labour of love that celebrates the comforting yet elegant flavours and rich traditions of modern Greek food.

My odyssey began in 2002, in the heart of New York City, where I enrolled in a culinary school to obtain my diploma in culinary arts and restaurant management. It was here, amid the hustle and bustle of Manhattan, that I discovered my passion for challenging conventions in the kitchen. Inspired by the eclectic energy of the city and fuelled by a desire to explore new culinary horizons, I set out on a journey of experimentation and discovery that would ultimately lead me to the forefront of avant-garde Greek cooking.

In 2009, I embarked on a ground-breaking venture that would forever change the landscape of how I imagined modern Greek cuisine: the opening of Funky Gourmet, my first restaurant, in the heart of Athens. The restaurant offered tasting menus made from imaginative dishes that defied categorization and strived to redefine the possibilities of Greek gastronomy. Along with this inventive approach to cooking and a commitment to pushing boundaries, the restaurant gained international recognition by collecting its first Michelin star in 2012 followed by a second in 2014, and these were retained throughout the restaurant's life. This decade of exploring and creating avant-garde Greek cuisine pioneered the movement of modern Greek gastronomy, encouraging new standards of excellence in modern Greek food.

At the heart of this philosophy is a reverence for the rich culinary traditions of Greece. I have spent years studying the flavours, ingredients and techniques that define Greek cuisine, paying homage to the time-honoured recipes and customs that have been passed down through generations. From the simplicity of a classic Greek salad to the complexity of a slow-cooked lamb dish, I have embraced the essence of Greek cooking, infusing each dish with authenticity and soul. But while I cherish tradition, I am also a firm believer in the power of innovation. In my kitchens, creativity knows no bounds, constantly pushing to explore new culinary frontiers and challenge the status quo.

Whether it's experimenting with unexpected flavour combinations in a meticulously designed tasting menu or crafting a dish with simplicity based on the finest raw produce, in our restaurants we always strive to create recipes that are as surprising as they are delicious – dishes that awaken memories and summon up emotions. Beyond any accolades, the greatest reward lies in the joy of our guests when they visit our restaurants to enjoy an unforgettable dining experience.

As I embark on this new chapter with the release of my first cookbook, I'm reminded of the journey that has brought me to this moment: one that has been marked by passion, creativity and an unyielding commitment to cooking delicious food. Drawing on my years of experience as a chef, as well as the timeless traditions of Greek gastronomy, the recipes in this book reflect the essence, the richness and diversity of modern Greek cooking. With a nod to tradition and a flair for innovation that honours the past, I hope that the recipes and stories featured in the following pages will inspire you to embrace the beauty and future of modern Greek food and to join us on this culinary adventure.

Welcome to our world of modern Greek food!

**NIKOS**

18  Tzatziki
20  Taramas
22  Fava
24  Ox Tongue Carpaccio
26  Metsovone Croquette
28  Feta Kataifi
30  Spanakopita

# The Greek Larder

# BAKALIKO

In Greece, a *bakaliko* (μπακάλικο) refers to a traditional neighbourhood grocery shop. A place where cured products, cheese and larder delicacies, such as legumes, olives and capers, were always on display. Cheese was usually made from goat's and sheep's milk; seafood was mostly cured sardines and other small cheap fish as well as *taramas* (the cod's roe used to make the famous Greek *taramosalata*). Fresh ingredients, such as yoghurt and seasonal vegetables, were also available, along with wine, distilled spirits and coffee, which they would grind on the spot.

However, it's not just the products that made these shops special – it's the sense of belonging that they evoke. Regular customers aren't just shoppers, they're family. Shopkeepers know their patrons by name, inquire about their family's well-being and welcome newcomers with open arms.

For generations, the *bakaliko* has been more than just a place to purchase food. Nestled right in the heart of neighbourhoods, it's the meeting point where locals gather to catch up on gossip, discuss politics, or simply share some strong Greek coffee or a few glasses of *tsipouro* or wine while nibbling on simple snacks and 'bites'. News is exchanged and friendships are forged.

With the rise of modern supermarkets and convenience stores, the number of *bakalika* has decreased, but they continue to play an important role, particularly in smaller towns, rural areas and some urban neighbourhoods. In our fast-paced modern world, these shops remain etched forever in the hearts of Greek people, preserving traditions and fostering connections that transcend generations. We honour the *bakaliko* and its speciality larder foods in the recipes featured in the following pages.

# Tzatziki

Famous all over the world, tzatziki takes centre stage on every Greek table. The creamy texture of double-strained Greek yoghurt is heightened by the refreshing cucumber while an infusion of garlic and extra-virgin olive oil adds depth to the flavour. Tzatziki is usually served as an appetizer with pitta or rustic sourdough bread, but it's also a great accompaniment to meat, especially in gyro wraps. We've tweaked the traditional recipe by delicately layering the cucumber on top at the last minute to preserve its cool, crisp texture, and roasting and puréeing the garlic for a lighter and more subtle taste.

**SERVES 4**

400g full-fat Greek yoghurt
40ml extra-virgin olive oil
1 tbsp sherry vinegar
½ garlic clove, finely chopped
a pinch of chilli powder
¾ tsp fine salt
1 tbsp garlic purée (*see page 270*)
grilled pitta bread, to serve

**GARNISH:**

40g cucumber, skin on, deseeded and finely diced
a pinch of dried dill
extra-virgin olive oil, for drizzling
a few tips of dill

Place the yoghurt, olive oil, vinegar, garlic, chilli powder, salt and garlic purée in a bowl and mix well.

To serve, spoon the tzatziki onto a plate and top with the diced cucumber. Drizzle with olive oil, sprinkle with the dried dill and garnish with the dill tips. Enjoy with some grilled pitta bread.

# Taramas

Let's start by differentiating between *taramas* and *taramosalata*. Taramas refers to the cured eggs of cod, whereas *taramosalata* is a spread made by blending the cured eggs with bread, olive oil, a hint of garlic and lemon juice. Although *salata* means salad in Greek, we often simply refer to this dish as 'taramas' when ordering it in tavernas. To give our version more depth of flavour, we use rye bread in the blending and top the final dish with the finest Greek bottarga to achieve a lingering aftertaste. Bottarga, another kind of roe widely used in Greek cuisine, comes from the 'bafa' fish, which is a local kind of grey mullet. By making this dish you will become familiar with these speciality Greek roe products, which are so deeply rooted in the culinary background of the country. Back in the old times, taramas was found in most Greek households, not only because of its salty and delicate fishy flavour but also because it was a cheap and easy way to enjoy a delicious, filling spread. For us it's a delicacy, especially as we use high-quality 'taramas' cod roe, peppery extra-virgin olive oil and Greek bottarga.

**SERVES 4**

- 70g two-day-old sourdough rye bread (see page 202), crust removed and cut into large cubes
- 160ml sunflower oil
- 150ml water
- 25g white taramas (100% cod's roe)
- 4 tsp extra-virgin olive oil
- 1 tsp lemon juice, strained
- grated zest of ¼ lemon
- ½ garlic clove, finely chopped
- a pinch of fine salt
- sourdough bread (see page 202), to serve

**GARNISH:**
- sunflower oil, for deep-frying
- 1 shiso leaf
- 1 slice sourdough bread (see page 202)
- 1 tbsp bottarga crumbled

Place the bread cubes in a bowl. Add the sunflower oil and set aside to soak for 10 minutes.

Transfer the bread and sunflower oil to a blender. Add the water, taramas, olive oil, lemon juice and zest, garlic and salt. Blend for 5–10 minutes, or until the mixture is smooth with a fine texture. Transfer to a bowl, cover and leave in the fridge until cold.

Just before serving, make the garnish: pour enough sunflower oil to deep-fry the shiso leaf into a small pan. Set over a medium to high heat and, when it's hot, add the leaf and fry for 10 seconds on each side, or until crisp. Remove carefully with a slotted spoon and drain on kitchen paper.

Toast the slice of bread until blackened on both sides.

Transfer the taramas to a serving plate and scrape the blackened crumbs from the toasted bread over the top to give it a charred flavour. Sprinkle with bottarga and garnish with the fried shiso leaf. Serve immediately with fresh sourdough bread.

**TIP:** When blending the taramas, you can add cold water, a few drops at a time, through the feed tube to achieve a silky texture.

# Fava

With its rich taste and creamy texture, yellow fava bean purée is a standout dish. It is served everywhere in Greece, and regions such as Santorini and Feneos are renowned for their fava production and take great pride in this culinary gem. In Greek traditional cuisine, it's customary to combine pulses with seafood, so being loyal to this food combination, we garnish our fava with paper-thin bonito flakes to add a subtle yet distinctive flavour of the sea.

**SERVES 4**

200g fava beans (dry weight)
1.5 litres water
½ red onion, thinly sliced
¼ fennel bulb, stems and base removed, and thinly sliced
80ml extra-virgin olive oil, plus extra if needed
1 tsp fine salt, plus extra if needed
4 tsp lemon juice, strained, plus extra if needed
sourdough bread, (*see page 202*), to serve

**GARNISH:**
2 tbsp finely diced red onion
2 tbsp finely sliced flat-leaf parsley
grated zest of ½ lemon
freshly shaved bonito *or* bonito flakes

Place the fava beans in a colander and rinse under cold running water until the water runs clear. Drain well.

Transfer to a saucepan and add the measured water. Set over a high heat and bring to the boil, then reduce the heat to a simmer and skim any scum off the surface.

When the water is clear, then add the onion and fennel and place a circle of baking paper on top of the surface of the water to form a 'lid' and prevent the water evaporating too fast during cooking. Cook over a low to medium heat for 25 minutes, or until the fava beans are cooked through and the vegetables are tender. Strain, reserving the cooking liquid.

Transfer the fava beans and vegetables to a blender or food processor. Add the olive oil, salt and lemon juice and blend until smooth and velvety. If the mixture is too thick, thin it with a little of the reserved liquid, but do not use too much – you need to end up with a firm and thick purée. Check the seasoning, adding more salt, lemon juice or oil if needed.

Spoon the warm fava into a serving dish and sprinkle with diced red onion, parsley and lemon zest. Garnish with the freshly shaved bonito or bonito flakes and serve immediately with sourdough bread.

# Ox Tongue Carpaccio

Boiled ox tongue has always been considered a delicacy in Greece and was greatly appreciated by our parents and grandparents. The ox tongue was simmered in water for a long time until well cooked and tender. The cooking water, became infused with a strong meaty flavour, and was then used for cooking pasta or rice. The key to this dish is to thinly slice the tongue after cooking. It is best enjoyed cold, but you can lightly grill the slices over charcoal or sauté them in a pan before layering on the plate.

**SERVES 2**

10 slices cured smoked ox tongue, thinly sliced (approx. 2–3mm thick)
a good pinch of sea salt flakes
a good pinch of freshly ground Madagaskar pepper
5 coriander leaves, to garnish

**TOMATO & CORIANDER SALSA:**
2 tomatoes
½ red onion, finely diced
5 tbsp extra-virgin olive oil
½ tbsp lime juice, strained
a small handful of coriander leaves, thinly sliced
a pinch of fine salt
a few drops of Tabasco

Make the tomato and coriander salsa: cut a cross in the bottom of the tomatoes and blanch in a saucepan of boiling water for 8 seconds. Remove and plunge in a bowl of ice,

Peel the tomatoes and cut into wedges. Remove the seeds and pat the flesh dry with kitchen paper. Then dice the flesh and transfer into a bowl.

Add the remaining ingredients and mix gently. Place in the fridge until ready to serve.

Make the tomato and coriander salsa: put the diced tomato, red onion, olive oil, lime juice, coriander, salt and Tabasco in a small bowl and mix lightly to incorporate.

Fan the ox tongue slices on a serving plate and season with the salt and pepper.

Arrange the tomato and coriander salsa on top of the ox tongue slices in the style of a wreath and garnish with the coriander leaves.

**TIP**: Cured smoked ox tongue is available in many delis and supermarkets, either whole or sliced, in vacuum packs.

# Metsovone Croquette

Cheese croquettes are usually richly flavoured hot appetizers with fillings made from a combination of different cheeses or from a specific cheese mixed with other ingredients. Our task was to create a croquette that would be based on a stand-alone cheese to showcase its taste and consistency when served hot. We wanted a cheese that was packed with flavour, so every bite would burst out into your mouth like an explosion. We chose Metsovone, a smoked cheese from Metsovo, with a distinctive rich, smoky flavour that goes well with sweet chutneys. Partnered with our unique and super-easy rhubarb jam, we ended up with an amazing cheese and jam combination.

**MAKES 1 PORTION (SERVES 2)**

50g plain flour, sifted
1 medium egg, beaten
30g panko breadcrumbs, blended to a fine powder
100g slice Metsovone smoked cheese (or any cylindrical smoked cow's milk cheese)
sunflower oil, for deep-frying
2 tbsp rhubarb jam (see recipe below)

**RHUBARB JAM:**
500g rhubarb, trimmed and peeled
250g caster sugar

To coat the cheese: place the flour, beaten egg and panko breadcrumbs into three separate shallow containers.

Lightly coat the cheese slice with the flour, patting it gently to remove any excess. Dip it into the beaten egg and then coat it all over with the breadcrumbs, pressing them gently onto the cheese to make them stick.

Dip the breadcrumbed croquette back into the beaten egg and then into the breadcrumbs for a second time.

Pour the oil – just enough to deep-fry the croquette – into a frying pan and set over a medium to high heat. Pierce through the croquette with a thin wooden skewer (this will prevent it puffing up and breaking during cooking) and fry it in the hot oil for 3–4 minutes, or until crisp and golden brown. Remove from the pan and drain on kitchen paper.

Serve on a plate with the rhubarb jam on the side.

**RHUBARB JAM**

Cut the rhubarb stalks into 3–4cm lengths and place in a saucepan with the sugar. Simmer gently over a low heat, stirring often, until the sugar dissolves and the rhubarb breaks into threads. Cook, stirring occasionally, for 30 minutes more, or until the mixture is thick and jammy.

Take the pan off the heat and set aside to cool at room temperature before spooning the jam into a sterilized jar with a screw-top lid. Cool and then store in the fridge for up to 1 month.

# Feta Kataifi

The tangy kick of salty feta cheese pairs wonderfully with sweet flavours, especially thyme honey. Inspired by classic Greek sweets of crispy filo soaked in a honey syrup, we've created a tasty savoury combo. We wrap our feta in crispy kataifi filo and fry it until golden, then add a drizzle of honey and a sprinkle of sesame seeds. A touch of lemon juice provides a refreshing contrast to balance the richness and sweetness.

**MAKES 1 PORTION (SERVES 2)**

50g kataifi filo (dry weight), defrosted
50g plain flour, sifted
1 medium egg, beaten
100g slice feta cheese
sunflower oil, for deep-frying

**GARNISH:**
½ tsp lemon juice, strained
2 tbsp thyme honey
½ tsp white sesame seeds

Roughly chop the kataifi filo and transfer to a blender. Pulse – do *not* blend – to break it into smaller pieces, about 2–3cm long. Place the chopped kataifi in a shallow container.

Place the flour in another shallow container, and the beaten egg in a third one.

To bread: lightly coat the feta cheese with the flour, patting it to remove any excess. Dip it into the beaten egg and then into the kataifi to coat it all over. Press it gently onto the feta to make it stick.

Pour some oil – just enough to deep-fry the feta – into a saucepan and set over a medium heat. When it's hot, add the feta and fry until crisp and golden brown all over. Remove with a slotted spoon and drain on kitchen paper.

Place the feta on a serving plate and drizzle first with the lemon juice and then with thyme honey. Sprinkle with sesame seeds and serve.

# Spanakopita

Pies are a staple in the regional culinary maps of Greece. Each region has its own local fillings and secrets for the handmade pastry. The favourite pie in nearly every region is made with seasonal greens and goat's cheese – usually spinach and feta. The Greek name for this delicious pie is *spanakopita*, and in our take on the traditional recipe we use a buttery pâte brisée dough, which has a great biscuity texture to complement the filling.

**SERVES 2**

2 tbsp extra-virgin olive oil
¼ red onion, finely diced
½ small garlic clove, finely chopped
1 spring onion, thinly sliced
150g spinach, trimmed and washed
20 mint leaves, thinly sliced
1 tsp lemon juice, strained
40g feta cheese, crumbled
a splash of single cream
1 tbsp beaten egg
a generous pinch of sea salt
3–4 twists of freshly ground white pepper

**LEMON YOGHURT DIP:**
2 tsp extra-virgin olive oil
a pinch of fine salt
½ tsp sherry vinegar
¼ small garlic clove, finely chopped
5g garlic purée (*see page 270*) (optional)
100g full-fat Greek yoghurt
½ tsp lemon juice, strained
grated zest of ¼ lemon, plus extra to garnish

**PÂTE BRISÉE:**
200g strong white bread flour (T55), sifted, plus extra for dusting
a large pinch of fine salt
100g unsalted butter, cubed, cold
1 medium egg, lightly beaten
4 tbsp cold water

**TO FINISH THE PIE:**
1 egg yolk
1 tbsp full-fat milk

Make the lemon yoghurt dip: place all the ingredients in a bowl and mix well. Cover and chill in the fridge until required.

Make the pâte brisée: place the flour and salt in a food mixer and, using the paddle attachment, mix well together. Gradually add the butter, a few cubes at a time, until the mixture has the texture of coarsely grated Parmesan. Add half of the beaten egg with the water and mix until you have a smooth ball of dough. If it's too dry, add a little more beaten egg.

Wrap the dough in some cling film and let it rest in the fridge for 1 hour.

Meanwhile, heat the olive oil in a saucepan set over a low heat. Add the onion and cook gently for 3–4 minutes, or until tender. Stir in the garlic and spring onion and cook for 1 minute. Add the spinach leaves and cook, stirring occasionally, for 3–4 minutes – just long enough for them to wilt but retain their lovely green colour. Transfer to a colander and set aside to cool and strain well.

When cool, transfer to a bowl, stir in the mint leaves, lemon juice, feta, cream and beaten egg. Season with salt and pepper and mix gently.

Preheat the oven to 160°C fan (180°C), gas mark 4. Line a baking tray with baking paper.

On a lightly floured surface, roll out the chilled dough until it is approximately 2mm thick. If it's sticky, you can roll it between two sheets of baking paper. The dough should remain cold throughout. Cut out two circles, each 20cm in diameter.

Place one circle of dough on the lined baking tray. Spoon the spinach filling over the top, leaving a border around the edge. Cover with the remaining circle of dough and seal the edges tightly with your fingers by folding the bottom edge over the top and pressing the edges together.

With a fork, pierce the top of the pie to allow the steam to escape during baking. In a small bowl, whisk the egg yolk and milk together and use to lightly brush the pie.

Bake the pie in the preheated oven for 25 minutes, or until the pastry is golden brown and the base and top are both cooked.

Serve the pie, cut into slices, with the lemon yoghurt dip, topped with grated lemon zest.

36 Dakos Salad
38 Charred Lettuce
40 Stuffed Courgettes
42 Smoked Broccoli
44 Beetroot Salad
46 Roasted Cauliflower
48 Spinach Rice Pilaf

# Salads & Vegetables

# COOKING WITH VEGETABLES

Vegetables and salads are an integral part of the Greek culinary identity and a cornerstone of its healthy Mediterranean diet. Bursting with vibrant colours and bold flavours, Greece boasts a plethora of vegetable-based dishes that are both nutritious and delicious. They demonstrate the country's culinary ingenuity and deep connection to the land. Whether it's *horta* (boiled greens dressed with olive oil and lemon), *imam* (a hearty roasted aubergine dish) or *spanakorizo* (a comforting spinach and rice pilaf infused with lemon and dill), Greek cuisine celebrates the versatility and abundance of seasonal produce.

An emblematic vegetable dish of Greek cuisine, and the most iconic tomato salad in the world, is the Greek salad (*horiatiki*). Made with juicy tomatoes, crisp cucumber, tangy feta cheese, briny olives and green peppers, drizzled with extra-virgin olive oil and sprinkled with dried oregano, it's a refreshing and satisfying dish that epitomizes simplicity and flavour. Every bite is a harmonious blend of textures and tastes, a celebration of the freshest ingredients that nature has to offer.

What sets Greek vegetables and salads apart is not only their taste but also their health benefits. This approach maximizes flavour while ensuring that meals are packed with vitamins, minerals and antioxidants, which are essential for overall well-being and longevity. The inclusion of olive oil, a key component of the Mediterranean diet, adds heart-healthy monounsaturated fats and enhances the absorption of fat-soluble nutrients.

Moreover, Greek vegetables and salads reflect the cultural importance of food as a communal experience. In Greece, meals are meant to be shared with loved ones, enjoyed slowly, and savoured with gratitude. Whether gathered around a rustic taverna table overlooking the sea or dining al fresco in a sun-drenched courtyard, the joy of eating fresh, flavourful vegetables and salads is a cherished part of Greek life.

# Dakos Salad

Greek salad, or *horiatiki*, reigns supreme among tomato salads. Originally from Crete, a Dakos salad consists of a large rye rusk, topped with grated tomato and feta cheese. Our version combines the key ingredients of the traditional *horiatiki* with the essence of Dakos: a satisfying crunch from the olive oil rusks. Choosing the right tomatoes and extra-virgin olive oil is the key to success, but it's the tangy feta cheese that binds all the ingredients together. We are proud of our close relationships with Greek producers and use a special barrel-matured feta, which is extremely soft with a creamy-chewy consistency. Even today, we are the exclusive importers of this special product into the UK. This was one of the first dishes we launched to make London diners familiar with an authentic Greek tomato salad combined with an artisan feta cheese. It has been a staple on our menus and remains a firm favourite among our regulars.

**SERVES 2**

20g capers
240g cherry tomatoes, halved
70g Kalamata olives, pitted and halved
50g olive oil rusks, broken into large pieces
¼ small red onion, thinly sliced
a generous pinch of fine salt
½ tsp dried oregano, plus a pinch for sprinkling
100g barrel-matured soft feta cheese (or any high-quality barrelled feta)
1 tbsp extra-virgin olive oil

**BALSAMIC DRESSING:**

2 tsp balsamic vinegar
1 tsp thyme honey
4 tbsp extra-virgin olive oil

Make the balsamic dressing: mix the balsamic vinegar and honey in a bowl and gradually drizzle in the olive oil, whisking constantly until well amalgamated, smooth and creamy.

Rinse the capers under cold running water for 5 minutes to make them less salty. Drain well.

Place the tomatoes, olives, rusks, red onion and rinsed capers in a bowl. Season with fine salt and dried oregano. Add the dressing and toss gently.

Transfer to a serving plate and top with the feta. Sprinkle with oregano and drizzle with the olive oil before serving.

**TIP**: While we prefer the milder flavour of olive oil rusks, any fresh and crispy rusk you can find will do the trick.

# Charred Lettuce

This recipe is the story of all the lettuce salads that have been served alongside every lemon-flavoured Sunday roast in every Greek household. Picture the classic green salad that typically accompanies lemon oregano chicken or garlic and rosemary-roasted leg of lamb: a chopped romaine lettuce dressed with extra-virgin olive oil and a generous splash of red wine vinegar, and garnished with spring onions and dill, served with a thick slice of feta cheese on the side. We have combined all these ingredients in one dish and enhanced the flavour by chargrilling the lettuce.

**SERVES 2**

- ¼ large iceberg lettuce, any broken outer leaves removed
- 2 tsp extra-virgin olive oil
- a pinch of fine salt
- 2 tsp sherry vinegar
- a pinch of sea salt flakes
- 25g feta cheese, crumbled
- a few sprigs of dill, chopped
- ½ spring onion, thinly sliced
- 1 tsp chive oil (*see page 266*)

Lightly brush the cut sides of the lettuce with olive oil and sprinkle with the fine salt. Try to brush some of the oil and salt between the leaves, without breaking the lettuce.

Grill the lettuce, starting cut-side down, on a barbecue over hot charcoal or in a cast iron skillet set over a medium heat, for 2–3 minutes on each cut side, or until the edges are just browned and the lettuce is starting to colour, then turn it over and cook the outer side for 2 minutes.

Remove from the heat and place on a tray. Drizzle the sherry vinegar between the leaves, together with the sea salt flakes, and crumble the feta over the top. Sprinkle with the dill and spring onion.

Place the lettuce on a serving plate and drizzle with chive oil. Serve immediately while it is warm.

# Stuffed Courgettes

Stuffed vegetables are a feature of many different food cultures. In Greece, *gemista* is a beloved dish, especially during the summer months when tomatoes, courgettes and peppers are in season. The rice filling has a rich and aromatic flavour enriched by the sweetness of the cooked vegetables. We make our *gemista* using *trahanas* pasta mixed with fresh raw tuna and herbs. The courgette shells are cooked al dente to retain a hint of firmness. The key to cooking green vegetables, such as courgettes, green beans and broccoli, is to strike a balance between achieving an al dente texture and removing their raw flavour without overcooking them.

**SERVES 2**

2 large round courgettes
50g trahanas pasta, sweet
50g fresh tuna fillet, finely diced
1 spring onion, thinly sliced
a few sprigs of dill, chopped
10 mint leaves, thinly sliced
10 flat-leaf parsley leaves, thinly sliced
2 tsp extra-virgin olive oil, plus extra for basting
1 tsp lemon juice, strained
grated zest of ½ lime
a twist of freshly ground black pepper
a pinch of fine salt
1 tbsp chive oil (*see page 266*)

**AVGOLEMONO SAUCE:**

3 tsp lemon juice, strained
3 saffron threads
a small handful of dill, chopped
½ tsp sea salt flakes
3–4 twists of freshly ground white pepper
2 medium eggs
200ml chicken stock, at room temperature (*see page 262*)

Make the avgolemono sauce: place the lemon juice, saffron, dill, salt and pepper in a bowl and suspend it over a bowl of iced water, with the bottom of the top bowl touching the water below.

Break the eggs into a bain-marie or a heatproof bowl suspended over a pan of simmering water set over a medium heat, without the bottom of the bowl touching the water. Add the stock and whisk until the mixture amalgamates and becomes frothy (80°C on a sugar thermometer). Note: if you are using a Thermomix, set it to 80°C and mix at speed 6 for 8 minutes until frothy.

As soon as it reaches 80°C, strain the egg mixture through a sieve into the bowl of lemon juice and herbs set over ice. Whisk constantly until the mixture cools down. Cover with cling film attached to the surface, and set aside at room temperature until ready to serve.

Cut the top off each courgette to make a 'lid'. Scoop out the flesh from the bottom part, so you end up with two hollow shells. Discard the flesh.

Blanch both parts (top and bottom) of the courgettes in a saucepan of boiling water for 2 minutes. Drain in a colander and then plunge them into a bowl of iced water. Remove, drain well and set aside.

Cook the trahanas in a saucepan of boiling water for 4 minutes (or as per the instructions on the packet) and drain well. In a bowl, mix the drained trahanas with the tuna, spring onion, chopped herbs, olive oil, lemon juice, lime zest and seasoning.

Baste the courgette shells with olive oil and grill on all sides on a hot charcoal grill or cook in a cast iron skillet set over a medium heat until you can see light grill marks. Remove from the heat and fill the courgette shells with the trahanas and tuna mixture. Cover with the 'lids'.

Place each stuffed courgette in the centre of a serving dish and pour the avgolemono sauce around it. Drizzle with drops of chive oil and serve immediately while the courgettes are warm.

# Smoked Broccoli

This beloved lightly boiled and smoked vegetable dish is perfect as a salad or side dish. In Greece, eating seasonal boiled vegetables is very common and they are known as *vrasta* (from the verb *vrazo*, which means 'to boil'). In tavernas, we always ask for the daily specials, especially the *vrasta*, and the owner will suggest seasonal options. In summer, we savour the sweetness of courgettes, the bitterness of wild greens, known as *horta*, and the freshness of long green beans, such as *abelofasoula*. As winter sets in, we delight in cauliflower, *stamnagathi* greens, carrots and, of course, broccoli, while boiled potatoes are a must all year round. Our recipe, which is inspired by these lightly boiled vegetables, uses a touch of smoke to enhance the broccoli's flavour and add a new dimension.

**SERVES 4**

1 head of broccoli, stem trimmed
½ cup oak smoking chips
1 tsp extra-virgin olive oil
a pinch of fine salt
a pinch of sea salt flakes
3–4 twists of freshly ground white pepper
2 tsp lemon juice, strained
grated zest of ½ lemon
4 tbsp herb oil (*see page 266*)

**GREEK YOGHURT WASABI:**

50g full-fat Greek yoghurt, strained
3g fresh wasabi, finely grated, through a Microplane or an "Oroshi" grater
¼ tsp lemon juice, strained
½ tsp extra-virgin olive oil
fine salt, to taste

Make the Greek yoghurt wasabi: place all the ingredients in a bowl and mix well. Cover and chill in the fridge until ready to serve.

Cut the broccoli down through the middle from top to bottom into two halves. Blanch them in a saucepan of boiling water for 4 minutes, then remove and plunge briefly into iced water. Drain well and dry on kitchen paper.

Place the broccoli in a deep, stainless steel container or a medium saucepan. Use some kitchen foil to create a small 'nest' and fill it with the oak chips. Place it in the container next to the broccoli and use a torch to light the oak chips. When they start to smoke, cover the container with two layers of kitchen foil and leave it to smoke for 10–15 minutes.

Remove the broccoli from the container and drizzle with olive oil. Season with the fine salt and place it on a preheated hot charcoal grill or with a splash of olive oil in a cast iron skillet set over a medium heat. Cook, turning frequently, for 4–5 minutes, or until tender and charred. Remove from the heat and place on a tray. Season generously with sea salt flakes, pepper, and the lemon juice and zest.

Pour 2 tablespoons of herb oil into the centre of a shallow bowl with a flat surface. Place a charred broccoli half on top and serve with a spoonful of Greek yoghurt wasabi. Repeat with the other broccoli half.

# Beetroot Salad

Every year on the 25th March, Greece commemorates two very special events, a religious one and a historic one. The Orthodox Church celebrates the Annunciation when the archangel Gabriel visited Virgin Mary and told her that she would become the mother of Jesus Christ. Although it falls within the 40 days' Lenten fast, it's the only day when the Church permits the fast to be broken with fish. Years ago, cod was the only fish that was widely available and affordable. People could enjoy it fresh or cured, depending on where they lived, on the coast or inland away from the sea. Historically, the same day is Greek Independence Day, which marks the Greek Revolution of 1821 and liberation from Ottoman rule. The national dish of the day is cod served with skordalia and beetroots. Inspired by the customs of the past, we removed the fish from the equation and have added pickled blackberries to create a winter salad.

**SERVES 2**

450g baby beetroot, peeled, stems intact and roots trimmed
a pinch of fine salt
2 tsp extra-virgin olive oil
a pinch of sea salt flakes
2 tsp sherry vinegar
3 tsp sherry caramel vinegar (see page 274)
8 walnut halves
a generous pinch of sumac
grated zest of ½ lime
7 red-veined sorrel or baby beetroot leaves

**PICKLED BLACKBERRIES:**

100ml water
2 tbsp sherry vinegar
2 tbsp rice vinegar
25g caster sugar
a pinch of fennel seeds
a pinch of pink peppercorns
a pinch of coriander seeds
1 star anise
10 blackberries

**SKORDALIA:**

80g sourdough rye bread, (see page 202), crust removed and cubed
6 walnuts
1 small garlic clove, finely chopped
80ml sunflower oil

Make the pickled blackberries: place all the ingredients, except the blackberries, in a saucepan and set over a medium to high heat. Bring to the boil, whisking to dissolve the sugar. Reduce the heat to low and simmer for 4 minutes. Remove from the heat, transfer to a container, and leave in the fridge until cool.

Strain the liquid into a clean container and stir in the blackberries. Cover and return to the fridge until you're ready to serve.

Make the skordalia: add all the ingredients in a blender and blitz until well blended – do not overwork it or it may curdle. Transfer to a bowl and cover with cling film, resting it on the surface of the skordalia to prevent a skin forming. Chill in the fridge until ready to use.

Meanwhile, cook the baby beetroot in a saucepan of boiling water for 7–9 minutes, depending on their size, or until cooked through. Drain in a colander and then plunge them into a bowl of iced water. Remove and drain well.

Season the beetroot with fine salt and olive oil and transfer to a hot charcoal grill or a cast iron skillet set over a medium heat. Grill, turning frequently, for 4–5 minutes, or until they are cooked and just tender.

Remove from the heat and place on a tray. Sprinkle with sea salt flakes and drizzle with sherry vinegar and sherry caramel vinegar.

Place the skordalia in a mound in the centre of a serving platter or large shallow bowl and arrange the beetroots on top. Drain the pickled blackberries and use as a garnish with the walnut halves, reserving one

100ml water
5 tsp extra-virgin olive oil
1 tsp sherry vinegar
a generous pinch of fine salt

to finely grate over the top. Sprinkle with sumac and lime zest, garnish with the sorrel or baby beetroot leaves, grate the reserved walnut over the top and serve while the beetroots are still warm.

# Roasted Cauliflower

When we were kids, we dreaded returning home from school to the familiar smell of boiled cauliflower salad. Little did we know that the culprit was being overcooked – the poor cauliflower simmering away for an hour or more, releasing its pungent aroma as if in protest. In the Peloponnese, roasted cauliflower with tomatoes is a classic dish and, inspired by this, we devised our own version, swapping tomatoes for curry powder.

**SERVES 4**

1 whole cauliflower (about 1kg), leaves removed

**CURRY MAYO:**
100g garlic mayo (*see page 270*)
20g full-fat Greek yoghurt
½ tsp curry powder
½ tsp sherry vinegar
a pinch of fine salt

**CURRY BUTTER:**
3 tsp garlic purée (*see page 270*)
½ tsp curry powder
1 tsp fine salt
160g unsalted butter, at room temperature

**PANKO MIXTURE:**
60g panko breadcrumbs
60g hazelnuts, roasted and coarsely chopped
1 large garlic clove, finely chopped
a handful of flat-leaf parsley leaves, thinly sliced
a generous pinch of fine salt
20g graviera cheese, finely grated
50g unsalted butter, melted

Make the curry mayo: mix all the ingredients together in a bowl until smooth. Cover and chill in the fridge.

Make the curry butter: whisk all the ingredients together in a bowl.

Preheat the oven to 170°C fan (190°C), gas mark 5. Line two baking trays with baking paper.

Make the panko mixture: spread the panko breadcrumbs out on one of the lined baking trays and toast in the preheated oven for 10 minutes, mixing occasionally, to evenly colour. Transfer to a bowl, and stir in the hazelnuts, garlic, parsley, salt and cheese.

Rub half of the curry butter all over the cauliflower and place on the other lined baking tray. Cover the cauliflower with more baking paper and two layers of kitchen foil.

Bake in the preheated oven for 1 hour 15 minutes, or until cooked through and al dente, then remove and set aside to cool. Discard the foil and baking paper coverings.

When the cauliflower is cool, rub the remaining curry butter over it. Stir the melted butter into the panko mixture and use to coat the cauliflower, pressing it gently onto the curry butter to make it stick. Return to the oven and bake for 15 minutes, or until the panko crust is crisp and light golden brown.

Remove from the oven and place the cauliflower on a chopping board. Cut it in half vertically through the stem. Spoon half of the curry mayo into the centre of a large serving plate and place one cooked half of the cauliflower on top of the mayo. Serve the other cauliflower half in the same way on a separate plate.

**TIP**: If you want to give the cauliflower a smoky flavour, cook it cut-side down for 2 minutes over charcoal on the grill.

# Spinach Rice Pilaf

Despite our parents' tales of Popeye and his spinach-fuelled strength, a dish of spinach rice did not win us over. Today it's one of our favourites and we have transformed it into a classic oven-roasted rice pilaf. We prefer to use long-grain white rice, but feel free to experiment with any variety – you may have to adjust the boiling time at the outset and the amount of stock. For a vegetarian twist, use vegetable instead of chicken stock, but make sure it's strong enough to infuse the rice and leave behind a delicious glaze.

SERVES 2

120g long-grain white rice (dry weight)
200ml chicken stock (*see page 262*)
½ tsp sea salt flakes
2 tsp lemon juice, strained

**SPINACH:**
1 tbsp extra-virgin olive oil
50g spinach, washed and trimmed
a pinch of fine salt
1 tsp lemon juice, strained

**GARNISH:**
7 chives, chopped
1 spring onion, thinly sliced
20g goat's curd cheese, cut into pieces
10g feta cheese, diced
1 tbsp chopped dill
grated zest of ½ lemon
7 nasturtium leaves
1 tbsp extra-virgin olive oil

Preheat the oven to 200°C fan (220°C), gas mark 7.

Boil the rice in a saucepan of lightly salted water for 15 minutes. Drain and transfer to a Dutch oven or ovenproof casserole dish that is large enough for the rice to just cover the bottom – this will help it to caramelize.

Add the chicken stock and sea salt and evenly spread out the rice. Cook, uncovered, in the preheated oven for 20–25 minutes, or until the stock has evaporated and the rice has caramelized around the edge. Remove from the oven and sprinkle with lemon juice.

Meanwhile, cook the spinach: heat the olive oil in a saucepan set over a medium heat. Add the spinach and cook for 2–3 minutes, or until it wilts. Remove from the heat and season with fine salt and lemon juice.

Arrange the wilted spinach on top of the rice. Garnish with the chives, spring onion, goat's curd, feta and dill. Sprinkle with lemon zest, garnish with the nasturtium leaves and drizzle with olive oil. Serve immediately.

## Raw & Cured

- 58 Sea Bass Imam
- 60 Prawns Mikrolimano
- 62 Grouper Avgolemono
- 64 Catch of the day Crudo
- 66 Tuna Ladolemono
- 68 Greek Salad Carpaccio
- 70 Squid Matsata

## Seafood to Share

- 74 Kakavia Fishermen's Soup
- 76 Eel Carbonara
- 78 Smoked Tomato Lobster
- 80 Tuna Parmesan
- 82 Octopus Stifado
- 84 Skate Wing Bottarga
- 86 Monkfish Fricassee

# Seafood

# EXPLORING GREEK SEAFOOD
A Culinary Odyssey

In Greek culinary traditions, seafood holds a place of honour, with many regional specialities showcasing the country's rich cultural heritage. Surrounded by the Aegean and Ionian seas, Greece is a treasure trove of diverse seafood delights.

Blessed with a coastline that stretches over 13,000 kilometres and encompasses countless islands, Greece's proximity to the sea has profoundly influenced its gastronomic traditions. The Greek peninsula boasts an abundance of fresh and flavourful seafood delicacies that have become an integral part of the nation's culinary heritage. From the bustling harbour of Thessaloniki to the rugged shores of the Peloponnese and the islands of the Aegean, every corner of Greece has its own unique seafood dishes, shaped by local traditions, flavours and years of coastal living. From plump and succulent shrimps harvested in the Thermaic Gulf, to the highest-quality langoustines from Evia Island in the Aegean, Greek seafood is as diverse as it is delicious.

The Cycladic islands are renowned for their iconic seafood dishes, notably lobster pasta, made with freshly caught local lobster, which is cooked to perfection and tossed with al dente pasta in a fragrant tomato sauce infused with herbs and spices. Meanwhile, the sea around the Ionian islands further west yields an abundance of tender squid, which is expertly grilled and served with a squeeze of lemon and a drizzle of peppery unripe extra-virgin olive oil, creating a dish that is simple yet sublime.

Beyond its exquisite flavours, fresh seafood is also celebrated for its myriad health benefits. Rich in omega-3 fatty acids, vitamins and minerals, seafood is a cornerstone of the renowned Mediterranean diet.

For Greeks, the act of sharing a meal of freshly caught fish or seafood is not merely a culinary experience, it is a celebration of community, family and the timeless rhythms of coastal life. A testament to the inseparable bond between Greeks and the sea that has sustained them for generations.

# RAW & CURED

The practice of curing fish and preserving seafood in ancient Greece was not only a practical form of conservation but also a culinary art form that added depth and flavour to the food. Today, the word most commonly used to describe this phenomenon is the Japanese *umami*. While modern refrigeration has largely replaced these ancient methods, the tradition of curing and preserving seafood remains an integral part of the Greek culinary heritage, serving as a link to the past and a testament to the enduring resourcefulness of the Greek people.

One of the most common methods of curing fish in ancient Greece was salting. Fishermen would catch an abundance of fish, typically small varieties such as sardines, anchovies or mackerel, and immediately salt them to preserve their freshness. The fish would be cleaned, gutted and then generously coated in coarse sea salt before being left to dry in the sun or in the cool, salty sea breeze. Once cured, the salted fish could be stored for extended periods without spoiling, making it an invaluable source of protein during times of scarcity. The preserved fish would often be traded or sold in local markets, providing sustenance to communities far from the coast.

Another common method of preserving fish was through smoking. Fishermen would hang freshly caught fish over open fires, allowing the aromatic smoke to penetrate the flesh and impart a rich, smoky flavour, which enhanced its taste and texture. In addition to salting and smoking, Greeks in antiquity preserved seafood such as octopus and squid through drying. These creatures would be cleaned and then left to air dry in the sun until they achieved a leathery but tender texture. Once dried, they could be stored for long periods and rehydrated as needed for cooking.

Even today, one of the most iconic sights outside a fish taverna or *ouzeri* (a traditional small eatery, where ouzo, raki and wine are served along with a variety of small dishes – *mezedes* – composed mostly of seafood delicacies) is the octopus hanging from lines or racks to dry in the sun. Drawing inspiration from these traditional preserving methods, we use a quick curing process to maintain the freshness of the ingredients and our dishes are served either raw or lightly cured to perfection.

# Sea Bass Imam

This dish originated from the trimmings of the grilled aubergines, used for our moussakas (*see page 100*). Our moussakas is incredibly popular and we grill a lot of aubergines every day. We prick them with a fork and after grilling them, we leave them to cool on a rack to release any excess liquid before removing the charred skin. We use only the flesh, but not the drippings and skin. One of our senior chefs decided to taste the drippings, and was surprised by the burst of umami flavour. Intrigued, we tried it too and were amazed and knew he had discovered something special. Immediately we started to experiment with this bittersweet broth. Instances like this make us try to extract the best possible flavours from every ingredient and take pride in our commitment to sustainability, ensuring that nothing goes to waste. We're excited to share with you the very first recipe we developed using this broth. This dish reminded us of the flavours of Imam Baildi, an eastern-inspired dish we frequently cook in Greece, so we named this recipe after Imam.

**SERVES 2**

- 2 large aubergines
- 2 tbsp full-fat Greek yoghurt, strained
- 2 tsp finely diced red onion
- grated zest of ½ lemon
- 4 twists of freshly ground Madagascar pepper
- 140g wild sea bass fillet, skinned and boned
- a pinch of fine salt
- 3 tsp lemon juice, strained
- 2 tsp extra-virgin olive oil
- a pinch of sea salt flakes

Preheat the oven to 180°C fan (200°C), gas mark 6.

Prick the aubergines several times with a fork and place them on a baking sheet. Bake in the preheated oven for 1 hour, or until very soft inside.

Place the aubergines in a colander lined with cheesecloth (muslin) and set over a bowl. Leave to drain for 30 minutes or until they have exuded all their liquid into the bowl below. Note: You can use the flesh for the moussakas recipe (see page 100).

Spread the Greek yoghurt over the centre of a bowl and top with the red onion, lemon zest and pepper.

Slice the sea bass fillet into thick 20g slices and season them with salt and lemon juice.

Arrange the fish slices on top of the yoghurt and then pour the reserved aubergine broth around the fish to cover the edges of the fillets. Drizzle with olive oil and serve.

**TIP**: Alternatively, you can grill the aubergines over charcoal for a smokier flavour.

# Prawns Mikrolimano

Mikrolimano – 'small port' – is in Piraeus and well known for its bustling fish restaurants and tavernas. Back in the 1960s, a new dish appeared on the menus: prawns cooked in a tomato sauce, then finished with feta cheese and parsley. It was served in a bowl that looked like a pan and they called it *sagani*. It became so popular that it quickly spread to other areas of the Greek mainland and the islands with the name 'prawns saganaki'. Inspired by its flavours, we created a raw version of the dish. Instead of cooked tomato sauce, we used freshly grated tomato and vinegar; we swapped the cooked prawns for lightly marinated raw Carabinero ones; and we replaced the parsley with basil and traded the melting cooked feta cheese for cold grated feta. A hearty fragrant dish was transformed into a delicate starter.

**SERVES 2**

6 Carabinero prawns, shelled, deveined and cut into medium dice (or any fresh red prawns)
a pinch of fine salt
grated zest of ½ lime
2 tsp extra-virgin olive oil
1 tsp lemon juice, strained

**TOMATO RIGANADA:**
1 extra-ripe, juicy tomato
a pinch of fine salt
a splash of sherry vinegar
1 tsp extra-virgin olive oil
a sprinkle of dried oregano

**GARNISH:**
¼ tsp extra-virgin olive oil
a few drops of chilli oil (*see page 267*)
a small pinch of sea salt flakes
a small piece of hard feta cheese
5 small basil leaves

Make the tomato riganada: coarsely grate the tomato and strain well in a sieve, stirring occasionally. Transfer the strained tomato flesh to a bowl and add the remaining ingredients. Mix lightly and then set aside.

Place the prawns in a bowl with the fine salt, lime zest, olive oil and lemon juice. Stir gently until the prawns are lightly coated all over.

Place the tomato riganada in the middle of a serving bowl. Arrange the marinated prawns on top.

Drizzle with the olive oil and chilli oil, then sprinkle with the sea salt flakes. Grate some feta cheese, using a Microplane grater, over the prawns, and garnish with basil leaves. Serve immediately.

**TIP**: If you place the feta cheese in the freezer a little while before serving, it will be easier to grate.

# Grouper Avgolemono

When creating new modern Greek dishes, we often draw inspiration from other cuisines that we enjoy. Inspired by Peruvian ceviche, we've replaced the *leche de tigre* (tiger's milk) with the Greek signature egg and lemon sauce (avgolemono).

**SERVES 2**

80g grouper fillet, cut into medium dice
a pinch of fine salt
120ml avgolemono sauce, room temperature (*see page 264*)
10 thin slices red onion
10 thin slices fennel bulb
1 tsp lemon juice, strained
grated zest of ¼ lemon
1 tsp extra-virgin olive oil

**CHARRED GREENS:**

50g chard, washed and trimmed
1 tsp extra-virgin olive oil
a pinch of sea salt flakes
2 twists of freshly ground white pepper
1 tsp lemon juice, strained

**GARNISH:**

a small bunch of micro rocket cress
3 nasturtium leaves
petals from 2 edible viola flowers

Make the charred greens: blanch the greens in a saucepan of boiling water for 1 minute. Remove and plunge into a bowl of iced water to chill. Drain and pat dry with kitchen paper.

Drizzle the greens with olive oil and grill over charcoal or sauté in a pan set over a medium heat for 3–4 minutes, or until just starting to char. Remove from the heat and roughly chop the greens.

Transfer to a bowl and season with sea salt, white pepper and lemon juice.

Place the diced fish in another bowl and season lightly with the salt. Add ½ tablespoon avgolemono sauce together with the sliced onion, fennel, lemon juice and zest, and olive oil.

Arrange the charred greens in a semi-circle around the edge of a serving bowl without touching the bottom. Carefully arrange the fish mixture on top of the greens and pour the remaining avgolemono into the bottom of the bowl, until it reaches the level of the greens.

Garnish the fish with the micro rocket cress, nasturtium leaves and viola petals. Serve immediately.

# Catch of the day Crudo

The simplest way to enjoy a raw fish dish. All you need are two basic ingredients: a very fresh fish and a good-quality extra-virgin olive oil, plus some fish filleting skills. This recipe works wonders with fish like mullet, bream and bass. There are two varieties of extra-virgin olive oil that we like to use for this dish: mild and sweet 'manaki' or peppery 'koroneiki'. Of course, you can use any good extra-virgin olive oil.

**SERVES 2**

130g red mullet fillets, skinned and boned
a pinch of fine salt
3 tbsp extra-virgin olive oil
1 tsp lemon juice, strained
1 tsp fresh thyme leaves
grated zest of ¼ lemon
a pinch of sea salt flakes

Place the red mullet fillets on a chopping board and, starting from the tail end, use a sharp knife to slice them very thinly – ideally, they should be translucent. If you wipe your knife with some damp kitchen paper between slices, it's much easier.

Take a long serving platter and arrange the slices, next to each other, to cover the whole surface. Season lightly with fine salt, then drizzle evenly with olive oil and lemon juice. Garnish with thyme leaves, lemon zest and sea salt flakes and serve immediately.

**TIP**: You can also use unripe olive oil but not too much or it will overpower the delicate taste of the fish – a drizzle is enough.

# Tuna Ladolemono

In Greece, particularly for charred fish dishes, the go-to dressing is always *ladolemono*, a combination of *ladi* (olive oil) and *lemoni* (freshly squeezed lemon juice). It's the simplest recipe for a dressing to accompany a delicate dish and to showcase the high quality of the fish, without overpowering its flavour.

**SERVES 2**

180g yellowfin tuna fillet
1 tbsp extra-virgin olive oil, plus extra for drizzling
2 tbsp lemon juice, strained
a pinch of fine salt
2 twists of freshly ground Madagascar pepper
a pinch of dried oregano
grated zest of ¼ lemon
2 chives, finely chopped
a pinch of sea salt flakes

**PICKLED MUSTARD SEEDS:**
1 tbsp yellow mustard seeds
100ml white wine vinegar
25g caster sugar
½ tsp fine salt
2 thyme sprigs
a small pinch of whole pink peppercorns

**EGG YOLK CONFIT:**
extra-virgin olive oil, enough to cover the yolks
2 free-range egg yolks

**FRIED CAPERS:**
sunflower oil, for deep-frying
15 capers, rinsed well under cold running water for 5 minutes

Make the pickled mustard seeds: place the mustard seeds and enough water to cover them in a saucepan set over a high heat and bring to the boil. Cook for 1 minute, then strain through a sieve and repeat the process five more times, starting always with fresh tap water, or until the seeds lose their bitterness. Depending on the mustard seeds you may need to do this up to ten times.

Add the remaining ingredients in a saucepan set over a medium to high heat and bring to the boil, whisking to dissolve the sugar. Remove from the heat, add the boiled mustard seeds and leave to cool before transferring to a container and leaving overnight in the fridge, covered with a lid.

Make the egg yolk confit: preheat an electric oven to 65°C fan (85°C). For a gas oven, aim for the lowest possible temperature, leaving the door slightly ajar. Pour some olive oil into a small shallow tray to cover the bottom. Add the whole egg yolks, taking care not to break them, and then add enough olive oil to cover them completely.

Bake in the preheated oven for 25–30 minutes, then remove and leave the yolks to cool in the olive oil. Set aside until needed.

When you're ready to prepare the dish, lightly brush both sides of the tuna fillet with olive oil. Set a frying pan over a high heat and quickly sear the tuna on all sides. It should be lightly seared on the outside but still raw in the middle. Remove from the pan and transfer to a plate. Cover and rest in the fridge until it's cold.

Meanwhile, make the fried capers: pour some sunflower oil – just enough to deep-fry the capers – into a saucepan and set over a medium to high heat. When it's hot, add the capers and fry for 1 minute. Remove with a slotted spoon and drain on kitchen paper.

When the tuna is cool, remove it from the fridge and, using a sharp knife, carefully cut it into very thin slices – wipe the knife with damp kitchen paper between slices to make this easier.

Fold the tuna slices over and arrange them in a circle on a serving plate. Drizzle with olive oil and lemon juice before sprinkling with salt, pepper, oregano and lemon zest. Carefully place the egg yolk confit on top and sprinkle with the chives. Drain the pickled mustard seeds and use as a garnish with the fried capers. Sprinkle with sea salt flakes and serve.

# Greek Salad Carpaccio

We drew inspiration for this dish after eating lunch at a taverna in Epidaurus that was renowned for serving the freshest fish. We ordered a beautiful grilled wild gilthead bream with Greek salad on the side. Towards the end of the meal the owner joined us for a glass of wine. When he noticed the last few pieces of fish fillet still on our plates as well as the juices from the Greek salad in the bowl, he took our forks and added the fish to the salad bowl: 'Let them soak for a bit and then taste it – you have saved the best for last.' And he was right; the flavour was amazing. Later, thinking back on that day, we recalled that the fish on our plates had gone cold, and so the idea for this dish was born. A carpaccio of raw fish topped with the condiments of a Greek salad.

**SERVES 2**

80g yellowtail fillet, skinned, boned and thinly sliced
a pinch of fine salt
1 tbsp extra-virgin olive oil
1 tsp lemon juice, strained
2 cherry tomatoes, thinly sliced
1 tbsp finely diced red onion
1 tbsp finely diced cucumber, deseeded
1 tbsp finely diced feta cheese
a pinch of sea salt flakes
a pinch of dried oregano
grated zest of ¼ lemon

Place the yellowtail fillets on a chopping board and, starting from the tail end, use a sharp knife to slice them very thinly – ideally, they should be translucent. If you wipe your knife with some damp kitchen paper between slices, it's much easier.

Arrange the fish slices on a round serving platter to cover the whole surface.

Season with fine salt, olive oil and lemon juice. Garnish with the tomatoes, onion, cucumber and feta. Sprinkle with sea salt flakes, oregano and lemon zest and serve immediately.

RAW & CURED

# Squid Matsata

We enjoy coming up with names for our dishes. *Matsata* is a handmade traditional pasta from the Cycladic island of Folegandros in the Aegean Sea. It looks like tagliatelle but is almost double the thickness. There was a time when we were obsessed with squid and were experimenting with different ways to cut and cook it in order to create new dishes. When we cut it into strips, we immediately thought of *matsata* and decided to make it look like a pasta dish.

**SERVES 4**

2 large fresh squid tubes, approx. 350g each
700ml water
a good pinch of fine salt
4 tsp extra-virgin olive oil, plus 2 tsp for the garnish
3 tsp lemon juice, strained
grated zest of ½ lemon
a good pinch of sea salt flakes
several twists of freshly ground Madagascar pepper
30g Ossetra caviar

**GARLIC SOUP:**

30g unsalted butter
¼ red onion, thinly sliced
25g garlic purée (*see page 270*)
300ml single cream
100ml water
½ tsp sea salt flakes
1 tsp lemon juice, strained
2 twists of ground white pepper

Make the garlic soup: melt the butter in a saucepan set over a low heat. Add the onion and cook gently for 6–8 minutes, or until softened and translucent – do not colour. Stir in the garlic purée, cream, water and salt, then increase the heat and bring to the boil.

Reduce the heat immediately and simmer gently for 20 minutes, or until the mixture thickens. Strain through a sieve, then stir in the lemon juice and season with white pepper.

Meanwhile, prepare the squid: wash the squid tubes thoroughly, removing and discarding the inner parts and the exterior membrane. Cut open each tube on one side.

Boil the water in a saucepan, then remove from the heat and transfer to a container. Plunge the squid into the hot water and immerse for 30 seconds.

Remove the squid and pat dry with kitchen paper. Lay it flat on a chopping board and cut it lengthwise into long strips, about 4mm thick. Transfer the strips to a bowl and season with fine salt, olive oil, lemon juice and zest.

Spoon the soup into four bowls and arrange the marinated squid in the middle – like tagliatelle. Season with sea salt flakes and pepper, then top with the caviar and drizzle with olive oil.

# SEAFOOD TO SHARE

The following recipes are inspired by the traditional fish tavernas, which offer a feast for the senses and celebrate the bounty of the Greek seas in all their glory. These charming humble restaurants, which dot the coastline of Greece, provide an opportunity to savour the daily catch in a convivial and unpretentious atmosphere. Their seafood specialities offer a glimpse into dishes that are as diverse as they are delicious while celebrating the timeless connection between land and sea.

In the beginning, you are presented with a menu that showcases the freshest catch of the day, often sourced directly from local fishermen. As you linger over your meal, you are transported to a world of good food and great company where conversations flow freely, punctuated by laughter, storytelling and the clink of glasses. Plates are passed from hand to hand, allowing everyone to sample a variety of foods, flavours and textures, highlighting the importance of abundance and the generosity of Greek nature. No matter the size of the catch or the number of guests, there is always enough food to go round, reflecting the spirit of hospitality that defines the Greek way of life.

# Kakavia Fishermen's Soup

Kakavia is a soup prepared by fishermen on deck, using the inexpensive fish they have caught, such as small rock fish, which are packed with flavour. This delicate fish broth has a secret: very little water is used to make the intensive flavoursome and concentrated fish stock. The cooking time is also very brief to ensure its freshness. This stock serves as an excellent base for many seafood dishes, or it can be enjoyed simply on its own as a soup by adding some sea salt, extra virgin olive oil and freshly squeezed lemon juice.

### SERVES 4

1.2kg wild sea bass (see note opposite)
2 tbsp extra-virgin olive oil
½ tomato, chopped
¼ red onion, chopped
½ celery stick, chopped
½ carrot, chopped
1 small garlic clove, crushed
750ml water
grated zest of ½ lemon
1 large sprig of thyme
2 sprigs of parsley

### SOUP SEASONING:

1 tbsp lemon juice, strained
2 generous pinches of fine salt
several twists of freshly ground white pepper
4 tsp extra-virgin olive oil

### FISH MARINADE:

3 tbsp extra-virgin olive oil
a generous pinch of sea salt
grated zest of ½ lemon
1 tbsp lemon juice, strained

### TO SERVE:

4 thin slices purple kohlrabi
extra-virgin olive oil, for drizzling

Rinse the fish bones thoroughly under cold running water and break the large ones into smaller pieces.

Heat the olive oil in a medium-sized saucepan and sauté the bones, head and tail over a high heat for 2–3 minutes. Add the tomato, red onion, celery, carrot and garlic and cook, stirring occasionally, for 2 minutes.

Add the water – there should be enough to just cover the bones – and bring to the boil. Reduce the heat to low and simmer for 20 minutes, skimming any foamy scum and impurities off the surface with a ladle.

Remove the pan from the heat and stir in the lemon zest, thyme and parsley. Cover with cling film and set aside to steep for 10 minutes. Strain the soup through some cheesecloth (muslin) layered in a colander into a bowl. Discard the bones and vegetables.

Transfer the strained soup to a clean saucepan and set over a medium heat. Cook until the volume reduces by one-third. Season the soup by adding lemon juice, salt, white pepper and olive oil to taste.

You are now ready to marinate the fish: cut the skinned and boned sea bass fillets into medium-sized dice. Place them in a bowl with the olive oil, salt, lemon zest and juice and mix gently. Do not over-work the fish.

Cut out four circular disks from the 4 kohlrabi slices with a 5cm biscuit cutter and, with a knife, make a straight cut from the centre of the disc to the edge. Fold each slice into a cone.

Plate a small pile (around 100g) of the marinated fish in the centre of a bowl. Pour some of the hot fish soup around the fish and drizzle with olive oil. Top with a kohlrabi cone and repeat three times.

**NOTE**: Ask your fishmonger to clean and fillet the fish, and to give you the head, tail and bones. You should end up with two fillets of 200g each plus 400g bones, head and tail.

# Eel Carbonara

Smoked eel, which is widely produced in Greece, is a delicacy with a pungent rich flavour that is often found in household larders and in all the neighbourhood *bakalika* shops. Some regions, such as Mesolongi in central Greece, are renowned for their charcoal-grilled fresh eel, enhancing its natural flavour with a rich smokiness. Mixing and matching international dishes with the customs and ingredients of our country, we came up with this variation on pasta carbonara, in which the fattiness and smokiness of the eel replaces the cured pig cheeks typically used in this Italian dish.

**SERVES 2**

250g hylopites pasta (dry weight)
2 medium egg yolks
120g graviera cheese, finely grated
5–6 twists of freshly ground Madagascar pepper, plus extra for garnish
2 pinches of fine salt
½ tsp lemon juice, strained
grated zest of ½ lime
120g smoked eel
10 flat-leaf parsley sprigs, thinly sliced

**EGG YOLK CONFIT:**
extra-virgin olive oil, enough to cover
2 free-range egg yolks

Make the egg yolk confit: preheat an electric oven to : 65°C fan (85°C). For a gas oven aim for the lowest possible temperature leaving the door slightly open. Pour some olive oil into a small shallow tray to cover the bottom. Add the whole egg yolks carefully to prevent them from breaking and then add enough olive oil enough to cover them completely.

Bake in the preheated oven for 25–30 minutes, then remove and leave the yolks to cool in the olive oil. Set aside until needed. When it's time to use the yolks, remove them from the oil carefully with a slotted spoon.

Cook the hylopites pasta in a saucepan of boiling water for 5–6 minutes (or as per the packet instructions), until al dente. Drain the pasta in a colander, reserving 200ml of the boiled water.

Put the egg yolks, graviera cheese, pepper and half of the reserved boiled pasta water in a bowl and whisk well.

Return the strained pasta to the pan with the other half of the reserved pasta water and set over a low heat. Stir in the egg and cheese mixture and mix until you have a smooth and creamy sauce. Season with the salt, lemon juice and lime zest. Remove from the heat and set aside.

Using a sharp knife, score the eel in a diamond pattern and then char with a blowtorch. Cut into smaller pieces of 2 x 2cm.

Transfer the pasta to a serving dish. Make a small well in the centre and carefully add the egg yolk confit. Arrange the eel on top of the pasta, sprinkle with the parsley and add a grind or two of Madagascar pepper. Serve hot.

SEAFOOD TO SHARE

# Smoked Tomato Lobster

In the Greek islands during summertime, lobster pasta with spicy tomato sauce reigns supreme as perhaps the most beloved dish of the season. Here we have substituted the pasta with barley and infused the dish with a smoked tomato sauce. The recipe for the smoked tomato sauce is used throughout the book and can be found in Basic Recipes on page 268.

**SERVES 2**

1 live lobster, approx. 700g
2 tbsp extra-virgin olive oil
30g unsalted butter, cubed
1 tsp lemon juice, strained
grated zest of ½ lime
a pinch of sea salt flakes

**BARLEY:**
2 litres water
120g pearl barley (dry weight)
150ml chicken stock (see page 262)
120ml smoked tomato sauce (see page 268)
30g graviera cheese, grated
50g unsalted butter, cubed
½ tsp sherry vinegar
a pinch of fine salt
3–4 twists of freshly ground white pepper
a few chives, chopped
grated zest of ¼ lime

To cook the barley: add to boiling water and cook for 35 minutes. Strain in a colander and rinse under cold running water. Reserve covered with tea towels.

Place the lobster on a chopping board and swiftly insert the tip of a sharp knife into the centre of its head cutting downwards. Twist the head to separate it from the tail Remove the claws and discard the head. Remove the rubber bands from its claws and insert a metal skewer along the tail to prevent it from curving during boiling. Boil the tail for 4 minutes and claws for 6 minutes. Plunge into a container of iced water, remove and pat dry.

Remove the metal skewer. Use a pair of scissors to cut along the underside of the lobster's tail shell, then remove the tail meat in one piece and set aside. Insert a skewer into the top of the tail where the vein is located and carefully pull out the vein. Pull the claws off the body. Carefully remove the meat by gently smashing the shell. To keep the claws in one piece, cut them open with scissors and wiggle the smaller hinged pincer out of each claw. Rinse the lobster meat and pat dry.

Add the boiled barley to a medium saucepan set over a medium heat, add the chicken stock and cook until it is all absorbed. Stir in the smoked tomato sauce, cheese, butter, sherry vinegar and salt and cook gently for 1–2 minutes until creamy and well incorporated. Remove from the heat, add the chives and lime zest. Keep warm.

Meanwhile, heat the olive oil in a pan set over a medium heat and lightly sauté the lobster meat on all sides for 2 minutes. Add the butter and baste the lobster for another 2 minutes. Remove the pan from the heat and add the lemon juice, lime zest, pepper and sea salt flakes. Brush the lobster with the juices from the pan.

Spoon the barley onto a serving dish and arrange the lobster tail and claws on top.

# Tuna Parmesan

We're always intrigued by international comfort signature dishes that are loved by a wide audience. They often prompt us to explore new approaches to classic recipes while respecting their origins. Sometimes we try to elevate a dish but more often we add a Greek touch of innovation to create something new. One such dish is veal or chicken Parmesan, a classic dish of Italian cuisine. Here we decided to substitute the usual chicken or veal for fish. To rebalance the flavours we used a mild aged graviera instead of the classic robust 24-month Parmesan, ending up with a final dish of great comfort but also elegance that introduces a new idea of using fish in a classic meat recipe.

**SERVES 2**

50g plain flour, sifted
1 medium egg, beaten
50g panko breadcrumbs
1 x 300g tuna loin steak, bone in
sunflower oil, for deep-frying
a pinch of fine salt
50g tomato jam (see page 269)
20g graviera cheese, finely grated
5 basil leaves

**BASIL PESTO:**
35g graviera cheese, finely grated
100g pine nuts
a pinch of sea salt flakes
2 twists of freshly ground white pepper
40g basil leaves
25g mascarpone cheese
70ml extra-virgin olive oil

Make the basil pesto: put all the ingredients into a blender and blitz for a few seconds. Scrape down the sides of the blender continuously until you have a smooth mixture. Transfer to a container and cover with cling film resting on the surface of the pesto to prevent a skin forming. Set aside in the fridge.

You're now ready to prepare and cook the tuna. Do the breading procedure: place the flour, beaten egg and the panko breadcrumbs in three separate containers.

Lightly coat the tuna steak with flour, shaking off any excess, and then dip it into the beaten egg. Transfer to the panko and coat it well on all sides, pressing the breadcrumbs gently onto the steak to make them stick.

Pour enough sunflower oil in a saucepan to deep-fry the tuna and set over a medium to high heat. When the temperature reaches 170°C (you can check this with a thermometer), add the breaded tuna steak and fry for 1 minute for medium rare, or until golden brown and crisp all over. Remove with a slotted spoon and drain on kitchen paper. Season with salt.

Spread on top of the steak in layers, first the tomato jam, then the basil pesto and lastly add the graviera. Use a blowtorch to melt the graviera or place the layered steak in a preheated oven at 160°C fan (180°C), gas mark 4 for 1 minute.

To serve, slice into 1cm-thick slices and arrange fanned on a serving platter. Garnish with basil leaves and enjoy.

# Octopus Stifado

Stifado is a dish of braised onions with a strong kick of vinegar and allspice. While hare and deep-flavoured meats are commonly cooked stifado, we have innovated the classic recipe by cooking octopus instead. Inspired by octopus *xidato* (vinegary octopus), which is a classic *mezze* dish, we decided to marry the flavours of onion stifado and octopus and added black-eyed beans, which always pair well with molluscs, and wilted greens for a touch of freshness.

**SERVES 4**

- 1 frozen octopus (2–3kg), defrosted in the fridge overnight
- 1 tsp whole black peppercorns
- 5 dried bay leaves
- 4 tbsp extra-virgin olive oil, plus extra for drizzling
- 4 tbsp sherry vinegar
- 4 tbsp sherry caramel vinegar (see page 274)
- 4 confit banana shallots (see page 271), halved
- 12 caper leaves, rinsed with water

**BLACK-EYED BEANS:**

- 200g black-eyed beans (dry weight)
- 4 tbsp extra-virgin olive oil
- ¼ red onion, finely diced
- 80g baby spinach, washed
- 1 tsp fine salt
- 4 twists of freshly ground white pepper
- 2 tbsp sherry vinegar

Cook the octopus: preheat the oven to 220°C fan (240°C), gas mark 8. Line a baking tray with baking paper.

Remove and discard the mouth of the octopus. Place the octopus with the black peppercorns and bay leaves on the lined tray. Cover with kitchen foil and bake in the preheated oven for 1 hour 15 minutes.

Remove the octopus from the oven and lower the temperature to 170°C fan (190°C), gas mark 5. Discard the foil and any liquid on the baking tray, and bake the octopus, uncovered, for another 15 minutes. Remove from the oven and allow to cool slightly before separating the tentacles into four pairs. Cut off and discard the head.

In the meantime, cook the black-eyed beans: fill a saucepan with plenty of water and bring to the boil. Add the black-eyed beans and bring back to the boil, skimming any scum off the surface. Reduce the heat and simmer gently for 30–40 minutes, or until the beans are just tender and al dente. Drain well.

Heat the olive oil in a frying pan set over a medium heat and cook the onion for 3 minutes, or until softened. Stir in the boiled black-eyed beans and cook for 2 minutes. Add the spinach and cook for 1 minute until wilted, then season with salt and white pepper. Deglaze with the sherry vinegar and remove from the heat. Set aside.

Coat the octopus tentacles with 2 tablespoons olive oil and grill on all sides over charcoal or in a cast iron skillet set over a medium to high heat for 6–7 minutes. Remove from the heat and drizzle with the remaining 2 tablespoons olive oil, sherry vinegar and the sherry caramel vinegar.

To serve, place the beans and two shallot halves in each bowl with a pair of tentacles next to them. Drizzle with the remaining olive oil and top with the caper leaves.

# Skate Wing Bottarga

A skate wing is perfect for pan-searing, especially when it is paired with the rich flavours of brown butter and salty capers. Santorini's renowned capers add a distinctive touch to this delicious dish. After cooking, we add the finishing touches with a topping of fresh bottarga and tangy lemon zest.

**SERVES 2**

300g skate wing, skinned and bone in
½ tsp fine salt
2 tbsp extra-virgin olive oil
60g unsalted butter, cubed
1 tsp lemon juice, strained

**GARNISH:**
a pinch of sea salt flakes
grated zest of ½ lemon
10 flat-leaf parsley leaves, thinly sliced
2 tbsp bottarga, crumbled
1 tsp capers, rinsed well under cold running water for 5 minutes

Season both sides of the skate wing with salt.

Heat the olive oil in a frying pan set over a medium heat. The wing has a thin fillet on one side and a thicker one on the other side. Add the skate wing to the pan, thick fillet side down, and cook until lightly browned, about 5–7 minutes depending on the size. Flip the wing over and cook on the other side for 1 minute.

Add the butter and tilt the pan to swirl it around until it melts and turns a light brown colour. Use a spoon to baste the fish with the brown butter for 2 minutes and then stir in the lemon juice.

Remove the skate wing from the pan and pat gently with kitchen paper. Transfer to a serving dish and garnish with sea salt flakes, lemon zest, parsley, bottarga and capers. Serve immediately.

**TIP:** Cook the fish on the bone for a better flavour.

# Monkfish Fricassee

*Achnisto* is a cooking technique that is widely used in Greece for steaming whole fish. The fish is baked in a covered container in the oven with just enough liquid to create some steam, so it cooks gently and retains its moisture. Vegetables, including onions, carrots and leeks, are also added to give sweetness. The fricassee of greens is a great vegetable side for steamed fish and in this recipe the way we cook the fricassee ensures that the greens stay fresh and retain their vibrant colours with a kick of acidity. Fish cooked in this way need to be high in gelatine content, like rockfish or monkfish.

**SERVES 2**

3 tbsp extra-virgin olive oil
1 white onion, thinly sliced
1 large carrot, thinly sliced
1 small leek, thinly sliced
10 cherry tomatoes
a pinch of fine salt
a few twists of freshly ground white pepper
300ml water
800g whole monkfish tail, scaled
a pinch of sea salt flakes

**FRICASSEE SAUCE:**
3 tbsp extra-virgin olive oil
½ red onion, finely diced
4 spring onions, thinly sliced
400g iceberg lettuce, thinly sliced
a good pinch of fine salt
200ml avgolemono sauce (*see page 264*), cold
2 tbsp lemon juice, strained
a handful of dill, stalks removed, chopped
5–6 twists of freshly ground white pepper

Preheat the oven to 180°C (200°C), gas mark 6. Line a shallow roasting tin with baking paper.

Heat the olive oil in a frying pan set over a medium heat and cook the onion, carrot, leek and cherry tomatoes for 5 minutes, or until softened. Season with fine salt and white pepper. Stir in the water and remove from the heat.

Transfer everything to the lined roasting tin and place the monkfish on top of the vegetables. Sprinkle the fish with sea salt flakes and cover the tin with kitchen foil. Bake in the preheated oven for 40 minutes.

Remove from the oven and carefully transfer the fish to a clean tray. Cover with kitchen foil to keep it warm and set aside.

Strain the liquid through a fine strainer lined with cheesecloth (muslin) into a clean saucepan set over a medium heat and cook until it reduces by half to a sauce consistency. Set aside, keeping warm to drizzle over the plated fish.

Make the fricassee sauce: heat the olive oil in a shallow pan set over a medium heat and cook the red onion and spring onions for 1–2 minutes, or until just tender. Add the iceberg lettuce and salt and cook gently for 3–4 minutes, or until the lettuce wilts. Lower the heat and stir in the avgolemono sauce gently so it doesn't curdle. Stir in the lemon juice, dill and, pepper and remove from the heat.

Transfer the fricassee to an oval-shaped platter and arrange the monkfish tail on top. Pour the reduced fish sauce over the fish and serve immediately.

SEAFOOD TO SHARE

92 Giouvarlakia Dumplings
94 Moussakas
96 Beef Cheeks Giouvetsi
98 Lamb Shank Trahanas
100 Lemon Oregano Chicken
102 Hunkiar Beef Shank
104 Chicken Okra

Meat

# MEAT FEASTS

Animal farming in Greece dates back hundreds of years. Today different regions specialize in specific types of livestock farming based on their unique geographical and climatic conditions.

Cattle and pigs are farmed primarily on the mainland of Greece where the animals have access to larger areas of cultivated pastures and natural vegetation. The mountainous terrains of northern Greece are the natural habitat of wild boars and hunting them is a traditional activity that helps manage their populations.

Greek farms have significant numbers of sheep and goats as the mountainous terrain (on the mainland) and the islands are less suitable for raising cattle. Sheep can easily graze on the rugged, less fertile landscapes that are common throughout the country. Although they look very similar and have some common characteristics, such as hooves and a similar diet, sheep and goats have stark differences that set them apart. Sheep younger than 12 months are referred to as lamb.

Cooking-wise, the significant difference between goat's and sheep's meat is their fat content. It is lower in goat's meat, making it tougher than lamb, making it more suitable for slow cooking. Lamb on the other hand, is perfect for cooking on a charcoal grill or roasting. Animals on the islands often graze on sparse vegetation, such as shrubs and herbs. This can result in meat and dairy products with unique flavours that are influenced by the local flora.

'The Greek word πανηγύρια (panigiria) refers to traditional festivals that are celebrated throughout Greece and especially on the islands. On the island of Ikaria, one of my favourite festivals takes place in the village of Christos on the 15th of August. Festivities start bright and early, with music, dancing and eating continuing well into the early hours of the next day. The locals gather early to light the fires below large pots and spits. The delicacy of the day is slowly braised wild goat that simmers for hours over a low heat. Locals know to arrive early to sip the flavourful broth, which is called πρόθεση (prothesi). I remember the first time I tasted it. I was amazed by the pure, concentrated flavour and couldn't believe that it came from goat cooked in only water with nothing else added. The locals explained that their wild goats are so rich in flavour that no additional ingredients are needed. When the goat is finally taken out of the pots, it effortlessly falls off the bone. It's simplicity in all its glory.'
**NIKOS**

# Giouvarlakia Dumplings

Giouvarlakia are savoury meatballs, shaped from minced meat, rice and herbs, then slowly braised on the stove and finished with avgolemono sauce. When we modernize traditional Greek dishes, we often deconstruct them and then reimagine them with a fresh feel, texture and presentation, while preserving their authentic flavours. Our lamb meatballs are light and flavourful, wrapped in dumpling skins as a substitute for rice starch in the original dish. The delicate yet rich avgolemono brings all the flavours together, and the finishing touch of trout roe introduces a surf and turf element.

**SERVES 2**

2 tsp lemon juice, strained
2 tbsp full-fat Greek yoghurt
120ml avgolemono sauce (see page 264), warm
2 tbsp red trout roe (or salmon roe)
12 tips of dill
2 tsp chive oil (see page 266)

**DUMPLINGS:**

160g boned shoulder of lamb, minced
2 spring onions, finely chopped
2 tbsp finely chopped red onion
½ tbsp lemon juice, strained
1 tsp beaten egg
½ garlic clove, finely chopped
a small handful of parsley, leaves finely chopped
a small handful of dill, finely chopped
a pinch of chilli powder
½ tsp fine salt
2 twists of freshly ground white pepper
12 dumpling wrappers (8–9cm gyoza skins)

Make the dumplings: place all the ingredients except the dumpling wrappers in a bowl and, using your hands, mix everything together until well combined. Do this gently without overworking the mixture.

Divide the mixture into 12 equal-sized portions (15g each) and roll into oval balls. Place each ball in the centre of a dumpling wrapper and enclose it, sealing the edges with a little water and crimping them by hand. Repeat with the remaining dumplings.

Place the dumplings in a steamer basket and steam over a pan of boiling water for 6 minutes. Alternatively, use a flat, round colander lined with baking paper and suspended over a pan of boiling water – take care that the water does not touch the bottom of the steamer basket or colander and that the dumplings do not touch each other. Remove the dumplings and drizzle with lemon juice.

Place the yoghurt in the middle of a serving dish and arrange the dumplings around it. Spoon the avgolemono sauce over the dumplings and garnish with the trout roe and dill. Drizzle with chive oil and serve.

**TIP**: When sealing the dumplings, make sure that no air is trapped inside them.

# Moussakas

This recipe is a modern take on one of the most famous Greek traditional comfort foods and it has been a staple on our menus for years. Moussaka is an iconic dish with its layers of fried aubergines, potatoes, meat ragù and a classic béchamel sauce. We've embraced a lighter approach in our version by opting for chargrilled aubergines, using only the flesh, to achieve a more delicate texture than that of traditional frying methods. Topped with a flavourful beef ragù and a light béchamel, then crowned with crispy potato chips, this is the perfect combination, with all the layered ingredients coming together in one bite.

SERVES 4

30g unsalted butter
3 tbsp extra-virgin olive oil
½ red onion, finely chopped
1 garlic clove, finely chopped
300g beef shin, minced
60ml chicken stock (see page 262)
240g canned chopped tomatoes
1 small cinnamon stick
1 tsp fine salt
1 tbsp caster sugar
2 tbsp sherry vinegar
3–4 twists of freshly ground white pepper
4 medium aubergines
200ml béchamel sauce (see page 265)
½ tsp sea salt flakes
40g graviera cheese, grated

POTATO CHIPS:
2 medium Cyprus potatoes, peeled (or any variety suitable for frying)
sunflower oil, for deep-frying
a generous pinch of fine salt

Heat the butter and olive oil in a saucepan set over a medium to high heat. Add the onion and cook, stirring occasionally, for 6–8 minutes, or until softened and translucent. Add the garlic and cook for 1 minute.

Stir in the minced beef and cook for 5–10 minutes, or until browned all over. Add the chicken stock, chopped tomatoes, cinnamon stick, fine salt and sugar and bring to the boil.

Reduce the heat to low and simmer, stirring occasionally, for 45 minutes, or until the liquid reduces and thickens to a sauce consistency. Add the vinegar and white pepper, and cook for 5 minutes, then remove from the heat and set aside to cool.

Make the potato chips: cut the potatoes into 2mm-thick batons, using a knife or a mandoline. Rinse them in a colander under cold running water to remove any excess starch, then drain and pat dry with kitchen paper.

Pour enough sunflower oil to deep-fry the chips into a heavy saucepan. Set over a medium heat and when it gets hot, add the chips to the pan (in batches, if necessary). Cook, stirring gently, until the chips are crisp and light golden. Remove with a slotted spoon and layer them on kitchen paper, seasoning with salt while they are hot. Set aside to cool.

Preheat the oven to 180°C fan (200°C), gas mark 6.

Prick the aubergines several times with a fork and place on a baking sheet. Bake in the preheated oven for 1 hour, or until the flesh is very soft. Alternatively, you can grill them over charcoal.

Place the aubergines in a colander and set aside for 30 minutes or until they have exuded all their excess liquid. When they are cool enough to handle, carefully peel off the burnt skin, keeping the flesh whole.

Place four biscuit cutters of 9cm diameter on a tray lined with baking paper. Place a peeled aubergine in each cutter and press gently to shape it into a disc.

Top each aubergine disc with the minced beef ragù and then a layer of béchamel sauce. Sprinkle with sea salt flakes and grated graviera cheese and bake in the preheated oven for 7–8 minutes, or until warm in the centre and browned on top.

Remove from the oven and transfer each moussaka ring to a plate. Carefully remove the baking rings and serve topped with crispy potato chips.

**TIP**: The chips will become slightly darker after removing them from the hot oil, so be sure to take them out of the pan when they become light golden brown.

# Beef Cheeks Giouvetsi

Giouvetsi embodies the heartiness of Greek cuisine. It's made with orzo pasta cooked in the oven alongside meats, such as roasted leg of lamb or a tomato beef stew, until softened and creamy. As the orzo slowly cooks with the meat, it absorbs the flavourful juices, yielding a melt-in-your-mouth dish bursting with savoury goodness. In modern cooking, orzo is cooked al dente but still creamy, and it's often combined with seafood or vegetables. We use beef cheeks, which are renowned for their tenderness. With careful trimming and slow cooking, they have a rich, comforting flavour.

**SERVES 2**

2 x 400g beef cheeks
½ tsp fine salt
4 tbsp extra-virgin olive oil
200ml water
1 red onion, roughly chopped
4 garlic cloves, finely chopped
300ml red port
1 rosemary sprig
50g butter, diced

**SALSIFY CHIPS:**

3 salsify roots, washed
1 litre sunflower oil
a pinch of fine salt

**ORZO:**

2 lemongrass stalks
50ml extra-virgin olive oil, plus extra to cover the lemongrass
30g red onion, finely diced
1 garlic clove, finely chopped
250g orzo (dry weight)
50ml white wine
750ml chicken stock (see page 262)
180g tomato jam (see page 269)
a knob of unsalted butter
1 tsp fine salt
4 twists of freshly ground white pepper

Preheat the oven to 200°C fan (220°C), gas mark 7.

Season the beef cheeks with salt. Heat 2 tablespoons olive oil in a pan set over a medium heat and sauté the cheeks, turning them occasionally, until they are nicely browned all over. Remove them from the pan and transfer to a small–medium ceramic casserole dish.

Deglaze the pan with the water and bring to the boil, scraping the bottom of the pan with a rubber spatula to disolve any brown bits. Pour over the beef cheeks in the casserole dish.

Heat the remaining 2 tablespoons olive oil in the deglazed pan and cook the onion and garlic over a medium heat for 5 minutes, or until tender. Transfer to the casserole.

Pour the port into the casserole together with just enough water to cover the beef, and add the rosemary. Cover with some baking paper touching the surface of the liquid and then seal the casserole with kitchen foil. Put the lid on and place in the preheated oven. Cook for 30 minutes and then reduce the heat to 170°C fan (190°C), gas mark 5. Cook for 1 hour 30 minutes, or until the meat is very tender.

Remove the lid, baking paper and kitchen foil, and add the butter. Cook, uncovered, for 15 minutes, or until glazed and reduced. Remove from the oven and set aside.

While the beef cheeks are cooking, make the salsify chips: using a vegetable peeler, slice the salsify lengthwise into long thin strips.

Heat the sunflower oil in a heavy pan to 160°C. Add the salsify to the hot oil and fry, stirring continuously, until lightly browned. Remove with a slotted spoon and drain on kitchen paper. Sprinkle with fine salt and set aside at room temperature in a dry place.

TIP: Make sure that you remove the salsify from the oil as soon as it is lightly coloured. Over-frying it will result in a bitter taste.

About 30 minutes before the beef cheeks are ready to serve, make the orzo: cut off and discard the root and top of each lemongrass stalk and peel away the tough outer layers. Finely chop the white stems, transfer to a small dish or jar and lightly cover with oil.

Heat the olive oil in a wide saucepan set over a medium heat and cook the onion and garlic, stirring occasionally, for 6–8 minutes, or until softened but not browned. Stir in the orzo and sauté for 30 seconds. Deglaze with the white wine and cook until it evaporates. Gradually add the chicken stock, in three or four batches, stirring constantly until the orzo is cooked al dente but still creamy (this takes 10–15 minutes). Gently stir in the tomato jam and lemongrass until well incorporated. Add the butter, season with salt and pepper and continue stirring until the mixture is very creamy.

Transfer half the orzo to a serving plate and arrange a beef cheek on top. Drizzle with some of the sauce remaining in the casserole and serve garnished with salsify chips. Repeat with the second beef cheek, sauce and salsify chips.

# Lamb Shank Trahanas

Trahanas is a traditional Greek ingredient made from wheat flour, eggs and milk, then fermented and dried to form small pasta-like granules or larger chunks. There are two kinds: sour and sweet, but, to be precise, the latter is not really sweet, just less sour! Trahanas can be cooked in a soup or served creamy as a starchy side dish or a starter. It's interesting as it looks like pasta but it's not, as it contains milk. Its flavour is strongly characterized by the quality of the ingredients used during production, and this is why it is made in the Greek countryside, where producers use their own milk and eggs to create a unique taste.

SERVES 2

1 lamb shank, approx. 450–550g
a pinch of fine salt
4 tsp extra-virgin olive oil
3 sprigs of rosemary
1 garlic clove
200ml water
30g graviera cheese
30g fresh black truffle, thinly sliced

**MUSHROOMS:**

2 tbsp extra-virgin olive oil
200g shiitake or king oyster mushrooms, cleaned, stalks removed and roughly chopped
½ garlic clove, finely chopped
3 sprigs of thyme
a pinch of fine salt
20g unsalted butter

**MUSHROOM TRAHANAS:**

2 tbsp extra-virgin olive oil
½ white onion, finely chopped
120g trahanas pasta, sweet (dry weight)
70ml white wine
400ml hot chicken stock (*see page 262*), plus extra if needed
20g graviera cheese, grated
30g unsalted butter
½ tsp fine salt
2 twists of freshly ground white pepper
½ tbsp finely chopped chives
1 tbsp thinly sliced tarragon
1 tsp lemon juice, strained

Preheat the oven to 180°C fan (200°C), gas mark 6.

Season the lamb shank with salt. Heat the olive oil in a pan set over a medium heat. Add the lamb and cook it for a few minutes, turning occasionally, until golden brown all over.

Add the rosemary and garlic and cook for 1 minute, then deglaze with the water, and scrape the bottom of the pan with a rubber spatula to dislodge any brown bits.

Transfer everything from the pan to a ceramic casserole dish, cover with baking paper and kitchen foil and bake in the preheated oven for 1 hour 45 minutes, or until the lamb is really tender. Discard the foil and baking paper, then return the casserole to the oven for 5–10 minutes, or until the lamb shank is nicely coloured. Remove from the oven and cover to keep warm.

While the lamb is cooking, make the mushrooms for the trahanas: heat the olive oil in a pan set over a medium heat and cook the mushrooms, stirring occasionally, for 4–5 minutes, or until tender. Add the garlic, thyme and salt, and cook for 1 minute. Remove from the heat and stir in the butter. Discard the thyme sprigs.

Make the mushroom trahanas: heat the olive oil in a saucepan set over a medium heat and sauté the onion until softened and translucent. Add the trahanas and sauté, stirring, for 2–3 minutes. Deglaze with the white wine and continue stirring until it has evaporated. Gradually add the chicken stock, in three or four batches, and cook, stirring often, for 8–10 minutes, or until the trahanas pasta is cooked and the sauce is creamy.

Stir in the cooked mushrooms, graviera, butter, salt and pepper and mix well. Remove from the heat, then add the chives, tarragon and lemon juice.

**TIP**: If you have a thermal circulator, vacuum seal the lamb shank in a plastic bag with 10ml sunflower oil and cook sous-vide at 82°C for 12 hours.

Transfer the trahanas to a serving bowl and place the lamb shank on top. Finely grate the graviera cheese (using a Microplane grater) on one side of the dish and arrange the sliced black truffle over the top.

# Lemon Oregano Chicken

Roasted lemon oregano chicken with baked potatoes is a powerful flavour combination which is deeply rooted in Greek gastronomy as well as our hearts. We all grew up eating it – it's the Greek equivalent of the Sunday roast. The usual side dishes are a generous piece of feta cheese and a fresh salad of cos (romaine) lettuce dressed with extra-virgin olive oil and lots of red wine vinegar, along with dill and thinly sliced spring onion. We like to serve ours with creamy mashed potato and grilled baby gem lettuce.

**SERVES 2**

2 x 180g supreme chicken breasts, skin on, boneless with wing bone attached and frenched
1 tsp fine salt
a twist of freshly ground white pepper
2 tbsp extra-virgin olive oil
100ml lemon-oregano sauce, room temperature (*see page 265*)
a small piece of feta cheese

**MASHED POTATO:**

400g potatoes, e.g. Desirée, peeled and cut into large dice
160g unsalted butter
40ml single cream
1 tsp sea salt flakes
2–3 twists of freshly ground white pepper
a pinch of ground nutmeg

**GRILLED BABY GEM:**

1 baby gem lettuce, halved
2 tsp extra-virgin olive oil
1 tsp sherry vinegar
a pinch of fine salt

Make the mashed potato: place the potatoes in a saucepan with enough water to cover them. Set over a high heat and boil until they are cooked through. Drain well, setting aside for 3–4 minutes.

Transfer the potatoes to a bowl and mash with a potato masher or a food mill. Return the mashed potato to the pan, add the butter and whisk until it's well incorporated and the mixture is creamy. Stir in the cream and season with sea salt, pepper and nutmeg. Cook gently over a low heat, whisking constantly until smooth. Remove from the heat, then cover and keep warm while you cook the chicken.

Preheat the oven to 170°C fan (190°C), gas mark 5.

Season the chicken breasts with salt and pepper. Heat the olive oil in an ovenproof pan set over a medium heat and cook the chicken, skin-side down, for 6–8 minutes, or until the skin is golden brown. Flip the chicken over and cook the other side for 4–6 minutes.

Place the pan in the preheated oven and bake for 12 minutes. Remove from the oven, set aside to rest for 3 minutes, and then slice the chicken breasts into 1cm-thick slices.

Meanwhile, make the grilled baby gem: drizzle each half with olive oil and grill over hot charcoal on a barbecue, or put them, cut-side down, in a cast iron skillet set over a medium heat. Cook for 1–2 minutes, or until lightly charred, and then turn them over and cook the other side for 2 minutes. Remove from the heat, drizzle with sherry vinegar and season with fine salt.

Place half the mashed potato in the centre of a serving plate and fan the slices of one chicken breast on top. Coat the chicken with the lemon-oregano sauce and top with the grilled baby gem lettuce. Using a Microplane grater, grate the feta over the chicken. Repeat for the second chicken breast and serve immediately.

# Beef Shank Hunkiar

Hunkiar is a beef stew served with aubergine purée, which originated in Turkey and made its way to northern Greece with refugees returning from Constantinople. It was a signature dish in an old taverna in Halkidiki and we would call ahead asking the chef to save some for us.

**SERVES 2**

2 x 300g beef shank steaks, bone in (osso buco)
½ tsp fine salt
4 tbsp extra-virgin olive oil
200ml water
1 red onion, roughly chopped
4 garlic cloves, finely chopped
300ml red port
1 rosemary sprig
50g unsalted butter, cubed

**AUBERGINE MASH:**
2 large aubergines (450g each)
100ml béchamel sauce (*see page 265*)
a generous pinch of sea salt flakes
2 tsp lemon juice, strained

Make the aubergine mash: preheat the oven to 180°C fan (200°C), gas mark 6.

Prick the aubergines several times with a fork and place them on a baking sheet. Bake in the preheated oven for 1 hour, or until the flesh is very soft. Alternatively, you can grill them over charcoal.

Remove the aubergines from the oven and leave until cool enough to handle. Cut them in half lengthwise and scoop out the flesh. Transfer to a strainer or sieve set over a bowl for 10–15 minutes or until they have exuded all their excess liquid.

Place the strained flesh, together with the remaining ingredients, in a blender and pulse until smooth. Set aside while you cook the steaks.

Raise the oven temperature to 220°C fan (240°C), gas mark 9.

Shape each steak into a round and secure with kitchen twine. Season with salt.

Heat 2 tablespoons olive oil in a pan set over a medium heat and sauté the steaks, turning them occasionally, until they are nicely browned all over. Remove and transfer to a small ovenproof casserole dish.

Deglaze the pan with the water and bring to the boil, scraping the bottom of the pan with a rubber spatula to disolve any brown bits. Pour over the steaks in the casserole.

Heat the remaining 2 tablespoons olive oil in the deglazed pan and cook the onion and garlic over a medium heat, stirring occasionally, for 5 minutes, or until tender. Transfer to the casserole.

Pour the port into the casserole together with just enough water to cover the steaks and add the rosemary. Cover with some baking paper touching the surface of the liquid and then seal the casserole with kitchen foil. Put the lid on and cook in the preheated oven for 30 minutes, then reduce the heat to 160°C fan (180°C), gas mark 4 and cook for 1 hour 30 minutes, or until the meat is very tender and melting.

Remove the lid, baking paper and kitchen foil, add the butter and cook, uncovered, for 15 minutes, or until the sauce is glazed and reduced. Take the casserole out of the oven and remove the twine from the meat.

Arrange half the aubergine mash in the centre of a serving plate and carefully place a shank steak on top. Spoon some sauce from the casserole over the meat. Repeat with the second steak.

# Chicken Okra

A traditional chicken okra is a braised dish cooked in a casserole on top of the stove. It's strictly seasonal, served in spring and throughout the summer. The difficulty with this dish is to bring out the natural sweetness of the okra and produce the right amount of the unique 'saliva' effect from this incredible vegetable.

**SERVES 2**

1 poussin chicken (350-500g), spatchcocked with frenched drumstick bones
a generous pinch of fine salt
2 twists of freshly ground Madagaskar pepper
2 tbsp extra-virgin olive oil
2 whole garlic cloves
1 sprig of thyme
a knob of unsalted butter
4 small confit shallots (see page 271)
150ml lemon-oregano sauce (see page 265)
1 tbsp chive oil (see page 266)

**TOMATO RIGANADA:**
1 large extra-ripe, juicy tomato
1 tsp extra-virgin olive oil
a splash of sherry vinegar
a sprinkle of dried oregano
a pinch of fine salt

**OKRA:**
300ml water
300ml white vinegar
300g okra
2 tbsp extra-virgin olive oil
1 tbsp sherry vinegar
½ tsp sea salt flakes
3 twists of freshly ground white pepper
1 tsp sherry caramel vinegar (see page 274)

Make the tomato riganada: coarsely grate the tomato and strain through a sieve for 10–15 minutes. Transfer the strained tomato to a bowl, add the remaining ingredients and stir gently until well combined. Set aside in the fridge until required.

Prepare the okra: place the water and white vinegar in a bowl and stir well. Add the okra and place a cloth on the surface of the water to keep the okra submerged. Leave to soak for 30 minutes – this will reduce the 'saliva' effect that is produced during cooking.

Strain the okra and cook in a pan of boiling water for 6–8 minutes, or until al dente. Drain in a colander and then plunge them into a bowl of iced water. They should be tender but still vibrant green and a little crisp when you bite into them. Drain, pat dry and transfer to a bowl. Alternatively, you can steam them.

Preheat the oven to 170°C fan (190°C), gas mark 5.

Season the chicken with salt and pepper. Heat the olive oil in a large ovenproof pan set over a medium heat. Add the chicken and cook, breast-side down, for 6 minutes, or until lightly coloured. Turn the chicken over and add the garlic, thyme and butter. Cook for 6–8 minutes, basting occasionally. Transfer the pan to the oven and cook for 8–10 minutes, or until cooked through and crisp and golden brown on the outside.

Meanwhile, drizzle the okra with 1 tablespoon olive oil. Grill, turning occasionally, over charcoal (or cook in a cast iron skillet set over a high heat) for 4–5 minutes, or until slightly charred. Transfer to a bowl with the remaining olive oil, sherry vinegar, seasoning and sherry caramel vinegar, and toss gently.

To serve, cut the chicken in half lengthwise and place in a serving dish. Arrange the okra next to the chicken and top with the tomato riganada and confit shallots. Coat the chicken with the lemon-oregano sauce and drizzle the okra with chive oil.

## Snacks & Sides
112 Dolmades
114 Grilled Feta
116 Squid Skewer
118 Octopus Dog
120 Red Mullet Pitta Wraps
122 Aubergine Imam
124 Smoked Potato Salad
126 Charred Long Beans

## Charcoaled Meat
130 Lamb & Eel Kebabs
132 DIY Gyros Wraps
134 Souvlaki
136 Ultimate Burgers
138 Veal Liver in Caul Fat
140 Coffee Beef Picanha

## Whole Fish
146 Charcoaled Turbot
148 Fish & Greens

Barbecue

# EMBRACING THE GREEK BARBECUE
*A celebration of food, friendship & flaming charcoal*

In Greece, the barbecue is a cherished tradition, a celebration of food, friendship and the timeless art of charcoal grilling under the Greek sun. It isn't confined to a specific location and doesn't require a significant event to be organized. Eating outdoors is a way of life, a chance to communicate with nature and to revel in the simple pleasures of good company and delicious food.

The best part of any barbecue is the point when it's declared open. Tables groan under the weight of *meze* platters, crusty bread and vibrant salads, while there's laughter and lively conversation among the guests, each vying for the title of the ultimate fire-maker and the best cook. As the flames crackle and dance, small treats begin to sizzle on the grill, tantalizing the senses with their savoury aromas. As the evening unfolds, the atmosphere becomes electric, fuelled by the warmth of good food and even better company. Immersed in the vibrant energy of the Greek barbecue, in this timeless tradition, every meal is a celebration. We have felt like this at every barbecue since we were children, and we still experience it as adults.

You can experience it too! The time has come to organize your own Greek barbecue. We have created some recipes that embrace our philosophy of grilling over an open fire, and in the following pages you'll discover the pleasure of sharing delicious grilled food with your family and friends in the traditional Greek way.

*'Barbecues are not only about the food – there's the joy of sharing it with others. They are a celebration of life, love, friendship and good company. They don't even have to be organized in advance – a good barbecue can be spontaneous and happen anywhere at any time of the day or week. I've enjoyed barbecues in the mountains of Florina in northern Greece when it's been snowing as well as on the beach for an impromptu lunch of "surf and turf" in the hot sunshine. My favourite barbecue was back in 2010 on the stern of a catamaran in the middle of the Aegean Sea just off the island of Milos on the bluest waters I have ever seen. The barbecue was lit to grill the freshest octopus, sea urchins and wild fish, which had been caught just a few minutes earlier.'*

**ANDREAS**

# SNACKS & SIDES

Barbecues are not just for cooking large cuts of meat or whole fish; they are also perfect for preparing an array of small snacks, starters and sides. The intense heat of the grill brings out the depth in foods, transforming simple ingredients into flavourful delights. Marinated meats on racks, skewered cuts, fresh seafood and seasonal vegetables catch the aromatic smoke as they grill over the hot embers.

This chapter demonstrates how good-quality produce can be quickly transformed into elegant small barbecue plates. Traditional recipes, such as dolmadakia and souvlaki, are revisited, while a generous slice of feta is placed on the grill and served with charred vegetables – a combination of flavours that explodes in the mouth.

Explore these recipes and give your barbecues a festive feeling. You'll be able to serve delicious grilled foods to your family and friends and embrace the joy of eating outdoors.

# Dolmades

We've been charcoal grilling for many years and have experimented with almost every imaginable ingredient. To our delight, we've discovered an array of wonderful flavours and dishes that take on a new dimension when kissed by the charcoal's heat, and the humble *dolmas* is no exception. The unique smokiness of charcoal infuses each vine-wrapped *dolma* with a deep flavour and character, bringing a new perspective to this traditional favourite.

SERVES 4

100g trahanas pasta, sweet (dry weight)
½ tbsp extra-virgin olive oil, plus extra for brushing
1 tbsp chimichurri (see page 272)
a small handful of mint leaves, thinly sliced
2 tsp lemon juice, strained
a generous pinch of fine salt
3–4 twists of freshly ground Madagascar pepper
20 vine leaves in brine, lightly rinsed under cold running water

Boil the trahanas pasta in a saucepan of boiling water for 5 minutes. Drain and rinse under cold running water to cool them down. Drain again and transfer to a bowl. Drizzle with olive oil and toss gently to prevent the trahanas sticking to each other. Leave in the fridge for 10 minutes, or until cold.

Remove from the fridge and stir in the chimichurri and mint, then drizzle with lemon juice and season with salt and pepper. Mix gently to incorporate.

Place a vine leaf (shiny-side down) on a flat work surface. Place 1 tablespoon of the trahanas filling on the centre of the leaf and near the stem. Fold the bottom of the leaf over the filling, then fold in the sides and tightly roll up. Repeat with the other leaves until all the filling has been used.

Brush the dolmades with olive oil and place on the bars of a grill. Cook for 1 minute on each side until lightly charred.

Transfer the dolmades to a serving platter and serve immediately.

**TIP**: You can substitute barley for the trahanas.

# Grilled Feta

When heated, feta cheese takes on a whole new character and texture, which can be enjoyed in a variety of dishes. It is transformed from its familiar tangy-tasting form when enjoyed cold and becomes chewy and comforting. Grilling enhances its strong salty, milky flavour, so that it pairs exceptionally well with a wide range of ingredients. Feta stands out and shines when it's combined with charred vegetables on a barbecue. The smoky flavours of the vegetables complement the richness of the cheese, creating a great contrast. Chilli peppers are a fantastic companion to feta, adding a spicy kick that binds all the flavours together.

**SERVES 2**

100g feta cheese, sliced
4 cherry tomatoes, halved
4 spring onions, cut into 5cm lengths
4 Padron peppers
2 tsp extra-virgin olive oil, plus extra for drizzling
½ tsp chilli crunch (see page 273)
½ tsp lemon juice, strained
a pinch of fine salt
a pinch of dried oregano

Place the feta on a metal tray lined with baking paper and place on the grilling rack of a barbecue above the hot embers for 7–10 minutes, or until the feta is warm and slightly softened.

Meanwhile, place the tomatoes, spring onions and Padron peppers in a bowl and drizzle with the olive oil. Place in a perforated pan and grill above the hot embers until charred. Return to the bowl and mix with the chilli crunch, lemon juice and fine salt.

Place the feta cheese in the centre of a shallow dish. Top with the grilled vegetables, then drizzle with some more olive oil and sprinkle with dried oregano.

# Squid Skewer

Squid, a versatile seafood, offers a range of culinary possibilities, from stuffing and frying to roasting or braising. Yet, there's something uniquely satisfying about the simplicity of grilling it over charcoal, which brings out its natural flavours. The aromatic basil pesto pairs surprisingly well with the mollusc, adding flavour and elevating it into a dish of great comfort that celebrates the essence of quality ingredients.

**SERVES 2**

1 fresh squid, approx. 500g
extra-virgin olive oil, for drizzling
1 tsp lemon juice, strained
a generous pinch of sea salt flakes
2 tbsp basil pesto (see page 272)

**TOMATO & BASIL SALSA:**
2 tomatoes
½ red onion, finely diced
5 tbsp extra-virgin olive oil
½ tbsp lime juice, strained
a small handful of basil leaves, thinly sliced
a pinch of fine salt
a few drops of Tabasco

Make the tomato and basil salsa: cut a cross in the bottom of the tomatoes and blanch in a saucepan of boiling water for 8 seconds. Remove and plunge into a bowl of ice.

Peel the tomatoes and cut into wedges. Remove the seeds and pat dry with kitchen paper. Dice the flesh and transfer to a bowl.

Add the remaining ingredients and mix gently. Place in the fridge until ready to serve.

Prepare the squid: wash the squid under cold running water and separate the head from the tube (body). Separate the head from the tentacles and discard the head. Pull the exterior membrane off the tube and discard. Pull out the innards and the shell (quill) and discard. Cut open the tube on one side and lay it flat on a chopping board. Pat dry with kitchen paper and cut into 3cm squares. Thread the squares onto a long, thin metal skewer and, lastly, add the tentacles.

Drizzle the squid with olive oil and grill over hot embers, turning frequently, for 5–7 minutes, or until cooked and tender. Do not overcook or it will be tough. Remove from the heat and drizzle with more olive oil and lemon juice, and season with sea salt flakes.

Spoon the pesto down the centre of a serving plate and place the grilled squid skewer on top. Top with the tomato basil salsa and serve immediately.

# Octopus Dog

Although hot dogs are considered an American street food consumed in baseball stadiums, the story behind them is very interesting and they have evolved from different cultures and migrations. We know that back in the first century AD, the Greeks and Romans enjoyed eating sausages. They made their way to Frankfurt and Vienna more than 500 years ago, but it was not until the late nineteenth century that they reached New York. A German immigrant is credited with serving the first hot dog in Brooklyn back in the 1870s. We love them and have tried various kinds of pork or beef sausages, mixed with herbs, spices and jams, to come up with our own special hot dogs. However, this is our favourite – a hot dog made with octopus!

**SERVES 8**

- 2–3kg whole frozen octopus, defrosted in the fridge overnight
- 1 tsp whole black peppercorns
- 5 dried bay leaves
- 2 tbsp extra-virgin olive oil, plus extra for drizzling
- 2 tbsp sherry vinegar
- 4 tbsp sherry caramel vinegar (*see page 274*)
- 2 baby gem lettuces, quartered
- ¼ tsp fine salt

**TO SERVE:**
- 8 hot dog buns (*see page 200*)
- 8 tbsp red pepper ketchup (*see page 273*)
- 8 tbsp garlic mayo (*see page 270*)

Preheat the oven to 220°C fan (240°C), gas mark 9. Line a baking tray with baking paper.

Remove the mouth of the octopus from the underside located where the eight arms meet. Place the octopus, black peppercorns and bay leaves on the lined baking tray. Cover with kitchen foil and bake in the preheated oven for 1 hour 15 minutes.

Remove the octopus from the oven and lower the temperature to 170°C fan (190°C), gas mark 5. Discard the foil and any liquid on the baking tray and bake the octopus for another 15 minutes.

Remove from the oven and allow to cool slightly. When the octopus is cool enough to handle, cut off and discard the head, separating the eight tentacles. Drizzle the tentacles with the olive oil.

Grill the octopus tentacles over hot embers for 2–3 minutes on each side, or until charred. Remove from the heat and drizzle with some more olive oil, 1 tablespoon sherry vinegar and the sherry caramel vinegar.

Season the lettuce quarters with fine salt, olive oil and the rest of the sherry vinegar.

Slit open the hot dog buns and drizzle them with red pepper ketchup and garlic mayo. Place a lettuce quarter in each one with a charred octopus tentacle on top. Drizzle with some more red pepper ketchup and garlic mayo and eat immediately.

# Red Mullet Pitta Wraps

In a departure from the traditional souvlaki offerings of gyros, pork skewers or beef patties, the contemporary Greek culinary scene is wrapping all kinds of food in pitta bread. Intrigued by this evolution we started to explore making wraps with fresh fish and our quest led us to Greek red mullet, renowned for its intense flavour and natural sweetness. In Greece the sunlight plays a pivotal role in enhancing the taste of marine life by promoting the growth of phytoplankton. This is the basis of the food chain and it supports a richer and more diverse ecosystem and makes our fish taste better than deep-water ocean dwellers. For these wraps, we pair the red mullet fillets with thin and elegant olive oil flatbreads from Rhodes known as ladopita. If you can't source these, use thin tortilla wraps.

**SERVES 2**

2 x 120g red mullet fillets, boned, skin on
extra-virgin olive oil, for brushing
a pinch of sea salt flakes
2 olive oil flatbreads (see above) or tortilla wraps
2 tbsp full-fat Greek yoghurt
2 tsp Dijon mustard (or mild mustard)
½ tomato, thinly sliced
¼ onion, thinly sliced
10 mint leaves, thinly sliced
10 flat-leaf parsley leaves, thinly sliced

Brush the red mullet fillets with olive oil and grill, skin-side down, over hot embers for 3 minutes. Remove from the heat and season with sea salt flakes.

Lightly grill the olive oil flatbreads for 10–15 seconds on each side, or until warm but not crisp – they need to be pliable to fold them around the filling. Remove from the heat.

In a bowl, mix the Greek yoghurt with the mustard and spread over the flatbreads.

Top each flatbread with a red mullet fillet, some sliced tomato and onion, and the herbs. Wrap the flatbreads around the filling and enjoy.

**TIP:** If red mullet is not available, a fresh and fatty white fish, such as wild sea bass or bream, is an excellent alternative.

# Aubergine Imam

Imam dates back to the Ottoman Empire and consists of aubergines and onions cooked with olive oil and finished in a rich tomato sauce on top of the stove. It was embraced enthusiastically in Greece where aubergines are abundant during the summer and are paired with local high-quality olive oil. In our reinterpretation of this historic dish, we grill the aubergines over charcoal instead of braising them on the stove. The onions are caramelized separately, and the tomatoes are charred to complete the dish, thereby staying true to the classic ingredients while introducing a modern smoky touch.

**SERVES 2**

1 red onion, sliced
6 tbsp extra-virgin olive oil
2 pinches of fine salt
1 large aubergine
8 cherry tomatoes, halved
a pinch of sea salt flakes
2 twists of freshly ground white pepper
1 tsp sherry vinegar
2 tsp sherry caramel vinegar (see page 274)
40g feta cheese, crumbled
10 flat-leaf parsley leaves, thinly sliced

Mix the onion in a bowl with 2 tablespoons olive oil and a pinch of fine salt. Transfer to a perforated pan and grill over the hot embers, tossing occasionally, until softened and smoky. Remove and set aside.

Pierce the aubergine a few times with the tip of a knife. Cut it in half lengthwise and deeply score the inner flesh in a diamond pattern. Brush each cut side with 1 tablespoon olive oil and place on the bars of the grill over the hot embers. Cook, cut-side down, for 4–6 minutes, then turn the aubergine halves over and cook the outer skin side for another 2–3 minutes. Flip again and cook the cut side for another 4–6 minutes. Continue flipping the aubergine until charred and softened, making sure the flesh side is cooked more than the skin side – about 20 minutes cooking.

Meanwhile, mix the tomatoes in a bowl with 1 tablespoon olive oil and a pinch of fine salt. Transfer to a perforated pan and grill over the hot embers until smoky and softened. Remove and set aside.

Place the aubergine halves, skin-side down, on a serving plate and season with sea salt flakes and white pepper. Drizzle with the remaining olive oil, sherry vinegar and the sherry caramel vinegar. Top with the grilled onions and tomatoes and sprinkle with crumbled feta and parsley.

# Smoked Potato Salad

There's no better side dish for a barbecue than a well-prepared potato salad. It's perfect with meat and fish, and great for vegetarians and vegetable lovers. Grilling the potatoes brings out a smoky and unique flavour as well as a slightly crispy texture. We mix them with pickled spicy peppers to transform a classic side into a standout dish that will elevate any barbecue menu.

**SERVES 4**

1kg baby new potatoes, skin on, halved
2 tbsp extra-virgin olive oil
a generous pinch of fine salt
10 jarred pickled spicy green peppers
4 tsp lemon juice, strained
a generous pinch of sea salt flakes
5–6 twists of freshly ground Madagascar pepper
4 spring onions, thinly sliced
3 medium gherkins, finely diced
½ small red onion, thinly sliced
a handful of flat-leaf parsley leaves, thinly sliced
40g feta cheese, crumbled

Cook the potatoes in a saucepan of boiling water for about 15 minutes, or until cooked through – they need to be tender but not mushy.

Drain in a colander. Keep them in the colander and shake vigorously for a few seconds to scrape and roughen the surface of the potatoes. This will make them crisp when they are grilled. Transfer to a bowl and add 1 tablespoon olive oil and season with fine salt.

Grill the potatoes in a perforated pan set over the hot embers of a barbecue, flipping them in the pan occasionally, until they are golden brown and crisp all over.

Grill the pickled peppers on the bars of the grill over hot embers until lightly charred.

Transfer the potatoes to a bowl and add the remaining 1 tablespoon olive oil, the lemon juice, sea salt flakes, ground pepper, spring onions, gherkins, red onion and parsley. Toss gently to mix.

Transfer to a serving plate and top with the crumbled feta and charred pickled peppers.

SNACKS & SIDES

# Charred Long Beans

When in season, long green beans are a burst of fresh, vibrant flavour. They can be enjoyed steamed, boiled or grilled, each method bringing out their unique taste and texture. In this recipe, we grill the green beans to add a smoky depth, and garnish them with freshly grated tomato, crumbled feta cheese, extra-virgin olive oil and a hint of mint. This delightful combination creates a perfect salad or a flavourful side dish, showcasing the beans at their best.

**SERVES 2**

250g long green beans, trimmed
2 tbsp extra-virgin olive oil
1 tsp sherry vinegar
a generous pinch of fine salt
2 twists of freshly ground white pepper
3 confit cherry tomatoes (see page 271)
20g feta cheese, crumbled
4 mint leaves

**TOMATO RIGANADA:**

1 extra-ripe, juicy tomato
a pinch of fine salt
a splash of sherry vinegar
1 tsp extra-virgin olive oil
a sprinkle of dried oregano

Make the tomato riganada: coarsely grate the tomato and leave to strain through a sieve for 5–10 minutes, stirring occasionally. Place the strained tomato in a bowl and mix lightly with the remaining ingredients. Set aside.

Cook the beans in a saucepan of boiling water for 6 minutes, then plunge them into a bowl of iced water. Drain and pat dry with kitchen paper.

Transfer to a bowl and coat lightly with 1 tablespoon olive oil. Grill the beans on the bars of a barbecue grill over the hot embers, turning occasionally, for 2 minutes, or until lightly charred. Transfer to a large bowl and mix gently with the remaining olive oil, sherry vinegar, salt and pepper.

Arrange the grilled beans on a serving plate in the shape of a wreath. Top with the confit cherry tomatoes, placing a little tomato riganada in between them. Sprinkle with the crumbled feta and garnish with the mint leaves.

# CHARCOALED MEAT

In Greece, where culinary traditions are as old as the gods themselves, there exists a time-honoured ritual that speaks to the very soul of the nation – grilling meat over charcoal. It's a practice steeped in history, where the ancient art of the barbecue meets the bounty of Greek produce, creating a symphony of flavours. And at its heart lies the unparalleled quality of Greek meat. From the succulent beef of Epirus to the tender pork of the Peloponnese and the robust goat of the Aegean islands, Greece boasts an abundance of premium meats that serve as the foundation of this timeless custom.

But it's not just about the meats themselves; it's also the method – grilling over charcoal. The aroma of smouldering coals, infused with the essence of olive wood and fragrant herbs, fills the air as the meats slowly sizzle and char over the flames to take on a depth of flavour and complexity that are uniquely Greek – bold, robust and memorable. The charred exterior gives way to a melt-in-your-mouth perfection, while the burning coal imparts a subtle smokiness that lingers on the palate long after the last bite is savoured.

In this chapter, we let the flames roar, for tonight we dine like gods on Mount Olympus in a celebration of the beauty of the Greek barbecue.

*'I cherish the memories and always smile when I recall these special moments of going on holidays with my parents and family. We spent nearly every Easter in Karystos, a beautiful small coastal town on the southern part of Evia Island in the Aegean. My parents had lots of friends there and on Easter Sunday, in the time-honoured Greek tradition, a fire would always be lit for the barbecued lamb on a spit. They started early in the morning and continued until late in the afternoon, and throughout the day they would cook five to seven lambs to feed everyone that was invited. Everybody wished each other happy Easter and had a glass of wine or two, along with delicious cracklings of lamb skin and tender slow-cooked pieces of meat pulled from the lamb while it was turning on the spit. Tables were scattered around for the elderly to sit down and gossip, but the rest of us were always gathered near the fire and the spits to make jokes, enjoy the wine and nibble on small bites of sizzled happiness.'*

**NIKOS**

# Lamb & Eel Kebabs

In our endeavour to introduce surf and turf to the modern Greek barbecue, we combine lamb with eel. These two flavours complement each other perfectly, creating a richly flavoured skewer that can be eaten as a starter or main course. The robust taste of minced lamb is elevated by the umami flavour of smoked eel, which acts as the 'salt' element of the dish. This is best enjoyed with refreshing Greek yoghurt and a dash of chimichurri sauce.

**MAKES 14 SKEWERS**

1kg lamb shoulder, minced
1 red onion, finely chopped
8 spring onions, finely chopped
1 small garlic clove, finely chopped
20g flat-leaf parsley leaves, finely chopped
20g dill leaves, finely chopped
2 tbsp beaten egg
2½ tbsp lemon juice, strained
a pinch of chilli powder
1 tbsp fine salt
½ tsp ground white pepper
extra-virgin olive oil, for brushing
280g smoked eel, cut into 14 strips
100g full-fat Greek yoghurt
2 tbsp chimichurri (see page 272)

Place the minced lamb, both onions, garlic, herbs, beaten egg, lemon juice, chilli powder and seasoning in a bowl and mix gently, without overworking, until well combined. Cover and rest in the fridge for 30 minutes for the flavours to develop.

Divide the mixture into 14 equal-sized portions and shape each one into an oval patty. Chill in the fridge for 1 hour before grilling.

Lightly brush the lamb patties with olive oil and cook on the bars of a barbecue grill over the hot embers, turning them occasionally, for 5 minutes, or until medium cooked and juicy in the centre.

With a knife, score a diamond pattern on each strip of smoked eel and char with a blowtorch. If you don't have one, place the eel strips on the grill for a few seconds.

Thread each grilled lamb patty onto a small bamboo skewer and place a strip of eel on top. Serve with the Greek yoghurt topped with chimichurri.

CHARCOALED MEAT

# DIY Gyros Wraps

Creating your own gyros at home is simpler than you might think. All you need is the right cut of meat and a sharp knife. Traditional gyros are layered flat chunks of pork, cooked slowly on a vertical rotisserie to achieve even caramelization of the meat, while rendering its fat. They are then sliced thinly and served hot and crunchy, adding a rich flavour to every bite. We experimented to find the perfect meat for making gyros at home, without a rotisserie, and concluded that the secreto cut from Ibérico pigs is the best meat-to-fat ratio and eliminates the need for additional fat trimming and ensures a succulent result. With just a few essential tools, including a perforated pan, this dish is not only easy to make but also a delightful addition to your barbecue repertoire.

**MAKES 10 GYROS WRAPS**

1kg Ibérico pork secreto, cut into 5mm-thick slices
2 tsp fine salt
1 tsp extra-virgin olive oil
2 tsp lemon juice, strained
10 olive oil flatbreads or tortilla wraps
3 large tomatoes, sliced
2 large red onions, thinly sliced
300g tzatziki (*see page 18*)
a handful of flat-leaf parsley leaves, thinly sliced
sweet and smoked paprika, for dusting

**SPICE RUB:**
3 tsp garlic powder
3 tsp dried oregano
2 tsp smoked paprika
1 tsp ground white pepper
½ tsp chilli powder
¼ tsp onion powder

Make the spice rub: mix all the ingredients together in a bowl and set aside.

Coat the pork slices with the spice rub and grill in small batches in a perforated pan on a barbecue above the hot embers, tossing them occasionally until cooked through and caramelized.

Transfer the meat to a large bowl and season with the salt, olive oil and lemon juice.

Lightly grill the flatbreads on the bars of the grill above the charcoal embers for a few seconds until warm but not crisp. Transfer them to a serving platter.

Arrange, in different bowls, the grilled pork, tomatoes, onions, tzatziki sprinkled with parsley and paprika. Build your own gyros wrap, using these ingredients, and enjoy!

# Souvlaki

For many years there has been a grudge between Thessaloniki in northern Greece and Athens in the south about one fundamental question: what is *souvlaki*? In northern Greece, *souvlaki* refers to small pieces of meat on a skewer, taking its name from the Greek word *souvla* (a spit). Meanwhile, people in southern Greece refer to souvlaki as the skewered meat (or pork gyros or beef patties) wrapped in pitta flatbreads and flavoured with condiments, such as tomato, onion and tzatziki. Who are we to settle this timeless debate? Our recipe simply calls for the ideal meat to be skewered and chargrilled, accompanied by a flatbread. You can decide whether you will wrap it or not and if you will align with the north or the south – either way, you'll be embracing the Greek way.

**MAKES 10 SOUVLAKIA**

**IBÉRICO SKEWERS:**
1.8kg Ibérico pork presa, trimmed
fine salt, for seasoning
warm flatbreads (*see page 212*)

**TO SEASON:**
lemon juice
sea salt flakes
dried oregano

**RIBEYE SKEWERS:**
800g prime ribeye, boned and trimmed
fine salt, for seasoning
warm flatbreads (*see page 212*)

**TO SEASON:**
lemon juice
sea salt flakes
dried oregano

**IBERICO SKEWERS:** Cut the pork into 60 small cubes of 30g each. Try to get the cubes more or less the same size to ensure that they cook evenly on the grill.

Take ten metal skewers and thread six cubes onto each one.

Season the skewers lightly with salt and place on the bars of a barbecue grill above the hot embers. Cook, turning occasionally, for 8–10 minutes, or until cooked through and slightly charred.

Remove from the heat and season with sea salt, lemon juice and dried oregano. Serve with warm flatbreads.

**RIBEYE SKEWERS:** Cut the ribeye into ten 80g slices, each 1cm thick. Thread each slice onto a metal skewer, weaving it in and out in a wavy pattern.

Sprinkle the skewers with fine salt and place on the bars of a barbecue grill above the hot embers. Grill for 2 minutes each side, then remove and season with lemon juice, sea salt flakes and dried oregano. Serve with warm flatbreads.

**TIP:** If you want to wrap the skewer in a pitta, add tzatziki, tomato and onion.

# Ultimate Burgers

Why is a burger included in a modern Greek cookbook, and what is the culinary heritage behind it, you may ask? Well, burgers are not traditionally Greek, but the culinary history of a nation is not set in stone and it is constantly evolving. Each generation leaves its mark, blending unique elements from past and present to shape the future of the cuisine. Burgers have become deeply rooted in the everyday gastro-preferences of modern Greeks, and we felt compelled to include our recipe in this barbecue chapter. The key to any good burger lies in the meat patty. After extensive testing (and tasting), our verdict is that the best beef burger is made with short rib, offering a deep flavour and an ideal fat-to-meat ratio that needs just the right amount of sea salt flakes to enhance its taste. Combine this with the sweetness of a tahini-infused brioche bun, the kick from the vinegary gherkins and the richness of the melted cheese, and you have the ultimate burger.

**SERVES 6**

1kg beef short rib, coarsely ground
1 tbsp sea salt flakes
12 slices Cheddar cheese
6 tahini brioche buns (see page 214), halved
6 large gherkins, sliced

**TARTARE SAUCE:**

200g mayonnaise
60g capers, rinsed well under cold running water for 5 minutes, then chopped
40g mild mustard
40g full-fat Greek yoghurt
½ tsp ground cumin
40g gherkins, finely diced

Make the tartare sauce: mix all the ingredients together in a bowl, cover and chill in the fridge until required.

In a bowl, combine the minced beef and sea salt flakes. Do this gently and don't overwork the mixture.

Divide the mixture into 12 equal-sized portions and shape each one into a ball. Place each patty between two baking paper sheets and use a burger press to flatten it; if you don't have a press, use a flat spatula instead.

Grill one side of the patties on the bars of a barbecue grill above the hot embers for 1 minute. Flip them over, grill the other side for 30 seconds, then place a slice of Cheddar cheese on top and leave on the heat for another 30 seconds for medium-cooked patties.

Place the halved brioche buns, cut-side down, on the grill above the embers for 1 minute to warm them through. Remove and spread each cut side with a heaped spoonful of tartare sauce.

Assemble the burgers: place two grilled patties, cheese-side up, one on top of the other, on the base of a brioche bun and add a sliced gherkin. Cover with the top half of the bun and repeat in the same way with the remaining buns.

**NOTE**: You can substitute burger buns for the tahini brioche buns.

CHARCOALED MEAT

Barbecue 139

# Veal Liver in Caul Fat

Much of our inspiration is drawn from the dishes served over the years in traditional Greek tavernas. One such enduring delicacy, which is still a staple in meat tavernas, is charcoaled veal liver wrapped in caul fat. The caul fat is combined with the liver's lean meat to give just the right amount of richness and caramelization when cooked over charcoal. As modern Greek gastronomists, we strive to keep our standards high and respect our recipes' origins. This is why we present some Greek foods exactly as they were served in the past, trying only to source the best ingredients for the recipe with the only modern element in the equation being ourselves.

**SERVES 2**

450g veal liver
50g caul fat in one piece
1 tbsp extra-virgin olive oil
a pinch of fine salt
1 tsp lemon juice, strained
a pinch of sea salt flakes

Rinse the liver under cold running water and pat dry with kitchen paper. Wash the caul fat well, and dry with kitchen paper.

Wrap the caul fat around the liver three times, then trim away any excess fat. Brush with olive oil and season with fine salt.

Grill the liver on the bars of a barbecue grill above the hot embers, turning it often, for 8–10 minutes, or until medium cooked.

Remove from the heat and set aside to rest for 3–4 minutes. Cut the liver into 1cm-thick slices and transfer to a serving platter. Serve sprinkled with lemon juice and sea salt flakes.

# Coffee Beef Picanha

Where rubs take precedence over marinades when preparing meat for cooking on the barbecue, coffee can be a key ingredient in spice mixtures. With its bitter taste and unique aroma, it's ideal not only for many types of meat but also for seafood. In this recipe, we have used ground espresso coffee to create a spice rub that pairs perfectly with semi-fat picanha, which can be cooked whole over charcoal and then sliced just before serving.

**SERVES 4**

2kg beef picanha (also known as rump cap)

**COFFEE RUB:**
4 tsp ground espresso coffee
2 tsp light brown sugar
1 tsp sweet smoked paprika
½ tsp fine salt
½ tsp ground black pepper
¼ tsp ground cumin
½ tsp ground cardamom

Make the coffee rub: mix all the ingredients together in a bowl and set aside.

If the picanha is very fatty, trim off and discard some fat to leave a layer approximately 5mm thick. Score the fat crosswise in a diamond pattern to allow the heat to pass through into the meat and cook it evenly.

Rub the coffee rub into the meat and fat, evenly coating the whole piece of picanha. You may have to press the coffee rub onto the meat to make it stick.

Grill the picanha on the bars of a barbecue grill above the hot embers, with the barbecue lid closed for about 40 minutes, or until medium rare, flipping the meat every 6–8 minutes, to ensure even cooking.

Remove from the grill and leave to rest for 10 minutes before slicing it into 1cm-thick slices. Serve on a platter with seasonal grilled vegetables.

# WHOLE FISH

For Greeks, the art of eating a whole fish is a cherished tradition that speaks to our deep-rooted connection to the sea. From seaside tavernas to family gatherings, the ritual of enjoying a whole fish is steeped in cultural significance as well as culinary delight. Served grilled, roasted or fried, whole fish is celebrated for its simplicity and purity of flavour. Whether it's tender *tsipoura* (gilthead bream), sweet flavourful *barbounia* (red mullet) or succulent *stira*, *rofos* or *sfirida* (grouper family), each variety offers a unique taste of the Aegean and Ionian seas.

Beyond its exquisite flavour, eating a whole fish is a communal experience that fosters conviviality and connection. Sharing a platter of freshly caught fish with loved ones is a time-honoured tradition, where conversation flows as freely as the wine, and the scent of olive oil and lemons fills the air.

Moreover, the practice of eating whole fish embodies the Greek philosophy of 'waste not, use all'. By consuming the fish in its entirety – from fin to gill – Greeks pay tribute to the bounty of the sea and the importance of sustainable living. The oldest members of the family would always save the best parts of the fish for us to try when we were children, and they were never the fillets! We were encouraged to eat the eyes so we could see better when we grew up, to suck on the heads of freshly grilled langoustines, to taste the cheeks of larger fish (the most flavourful part of the fish head), and to eat tiny fried red mullets whole, including the spines and bones. These fish, perhaps the sweetest and most savoury from the depths of the Greek seas, were a true delight.

# Charcoaled Turbot

Grilling a whole fish on a barbecue brings out a depth of flavour that's hard to beat. And you can grill a wide array of vegetables simultaneously, creating a delicious and colourful medley to accompany the fish. The key to this dish is selecting a large, fresh fish, which can be perfectly caramelized over the charcoal, while the vegetables absorb the smoky aroma and enhance the overall experience. The possibilities are endless, and the result is a harmonious blend of smoky, savoury and fresh flavours that epitomize the joy of outdoor cooking. Our recipe calls for turbot with tomatoes and onions, but you can grill any flat fish over charcoal and serve it with your favourite vegetables and toppings.

**SERVES 2**

1kg wild turbot, skin on, scaled and gutted
extra-virgin olive oil, for brushing
fine salt, for seasoning
sea salt flakes
5 confit pearl onions (*see page 271*)
5 confit cherry tomatoes (*see page 271*)

Brush the fish with olive oil and season with fine salt.

Put on a fish grill cage and place over glowing embers, ideally 30–40cm above the charcoal. Grill, turning the fish once every 5 minutes, for 20–30 minutes, or until it is evenly coloured and the internal temperature reaches 45°C (test by inserting a digital thermometer probe).

Remove from the heat and leave to rest for 5 minutes. Season with sea salt flakes.

While the fish is resting, place the confit pearl onions and cherry tomatoes in a perforated pan and smoke them for 5 minutes over the embers, tossing gently.

Transfer the fish to a serving platter and arrange the smoked vegetables on top. Serve immediately.

# Fish & Greens

Greece boasts an incredible diversity of wild greens, reflecting its varied landscapes and rich biodiversity. From its mountainous woodlands to its sunny coasts, there's a wide variety of greens, each bringing unique flavours and nutritional benefits to the table. Woodlands provide robust plants like dandelion leaves and chicory, while the coast offers succulent, saline varieties such as monk's beard and sea fennel. In this recipe, a whole fish is carefully skewered on a spit to slowly rotate over the glowing charcoal, coaxing out its natural juices and adding smokiness to its flesh. A handful of monk's beard is lightly charred and delicately drizzled with olive oil and lemon juice – the quintessence of Greek cuisine.

**SERVES 2**

1.5kg whole wild sea bass, skin on, scaled and gutted
extra-virgin olive oil, for brushing
fine salt, for seasoning

**GREENS:**

300g monk's beard, cleaned and washed (or any chard, e.g. Swiss chard)
3 tbsp extra-virgin olive oil
a few pinches of sea salt flakes
2 twists of freshly ground white pepper
juice of 1 lemon, strained
grated zest of 1 lemon

Brush the sea bass generously with olive oil – this will help to keep it moist and prevent it sticking to the spit. Season evenly inside and outside with salt.

Carefully skewer the fish onto a spit, ensuring that it is centred and securely fastened. Place the spit over a charcoal grill, about 40cm above the fire, and start the rotisserie motor. If you don't have a rotisserie, place the spit at the same height and flip the fish every 5 minutes, so it cooks evenly on all sides.

Cook slowly for 30–40 minutes, or until the skin is evenly coloured and the internal temperature reaches 45°C (you can check this by inserting a digital thermometer probe). Remove the fish from the spit and set aside to rest for 5 minutes.

While the fish is cooking, make the greens: blanch them in a saucepan of boiling water for 1 minute 30 seconds. Plunge them into a bowl of iced water to cool them down. Drain and pat dry with kitchen paper.

Toss the greens in a bowl with 1 tablespoon olive oil and then grill in a perforated pan or on the bars of the grill above the hot embers, tossing occasionally, until slightly charred.

Transfer the greens to a bowl and season with salt, pepper, lemon juice, lemon zest and the remaining 2 tablespoons olive oil. Plate in a bowl, set aside and keep warm.

Carve the sea bass, discarding the spine but keeping the head and 'collars' (the meaty triangle between the gills and the rest of the body). Transfer the fillets, head and collars to a serving platter and serve with the greens on the side.

WHOLE FISH

## Breakfast
156 Greek Yoghurt & Toppings
160 Pancakes
164 Greek Toast
168 Rizogalo Brûlée

## Eggs
172 Village Eggs
174 Greek Eggs Benedict & Royale
178 Green Kayanas
180 Mountain Eggs
182 Open Pitta Lamb
184 Eggs Saganaki

## Bowls
188 Spicy Chicken Bowl
190 Tuna Bowl
192 Kale & Feta Bowl

# Greek Brunch

# BRUNCH

In this chapter, we introduce you to the modern Greek brunch, an idea we brought to London's dining scene in 2014 with the opening of our restaurant, OPSO. Since then, we've continuously built upon and evolved this philosophy. As you explore the recipes, you'll find some that are quick and easy to prepare, while others may appear more complex and time-consuming. Don't be discouraged – each recipe is achievable and well worth the effort. These dishes are perfect for cooking for family and friends. You'll find some familiar favourites and be surprised and delighted by new creations.

*'There is nothing like the feeling of contributing to your country's culinary heritage by introducing and establishing a new food habit that has come to stay.'*

**ANDREAS & NIKOS**

# BREAKFAST

In this chapter, you will find breakfast recipes that we have tested and tasted hundreds of times to elevate the humble Greek breakfast into a special experience. You'll discover modern Greek takes on pancakes, as well as breakfast classics reimagined, including the transformation of French toast into Greek toast, and rice porridge into a velvety *rizogalo* bowl.

'Back in 2012 I went through a phase of trying to find the best granola and the best eggs in London and it suddenly struck me one day, like a ton of bricks, that there was nothing on offer like the summer breakfasts we enjoyed in Greece. The idea of the modern Greek brunch was developed and when we opened OPSO in 2014, we decided to take it one step further by introducing Greek produce and customs into London's dining scene. Our dream came true, and we have now established the modern Greek brunch as an eating philosophy as well as an integral part of our restaurant's offering, much to the delight of our guests.'

**ANDREAS**

# Greek Yoghurt & Toppings

What makes Greek yoghurt so special? It's the high quality of the milk and the unique production method. The procedure of 'double straining' removes most of the whey, resulting in a thicker and creamier texture than yoghurt produced in other countries. It's perfect for any time of the day: kickstart your morning with a bowl of Greek yoghurt topped with fresh fruits and nuts, drizzled with honey; or enjoy it in traditional Greek dishes like tzatziki, or as an accompaniment to savoury dishes. Its high protein content makes it a good choice for a satisfying and healthy late-night snack. Here we share a selection of yoghurt toppings for breakfast as well as our signature granola recipe, which has won numerous awards in London's best breakfast choices.

**SERVES 1**

**TO SERVE (1 SERVING):**
- 200g full-fat Greek yoghurt
- 3 tbsp thyme honey
- 120g granola
- 60g fresh blueberries, frozen for 10–15 minutes in the freezer
- 1 tbsp pomegranate seeds
- 1 tbsp dark chocolate pearls
- 5 mint leaves, thinly sliced

**HAZELNUT CRUMBLE:**
- 100g unsalted butter, cubed
- 100g soft light brown sugar
- 30g caster sugar
- 1 tsp vanilla extract with seeds
- 1 tsp ground cinnamon
- a pinch of ground nutmeg
- 100g plain flour, sifted
- 180g roasted hazelnuts, roughly chopped

**GRANOLA TOPPING:**
- 250g jumbo oats, toasted in a preheated oven at 180°C fan (200°C), gas mark 6 for 10 minutes
- 250g dried cranberries
- 250g dried blueberries
- 250g cocoa nibs
- 250g hazelnuts, roasted in a preheated oven at 180°C fan (200°C), gas mark 6 for 7 minutes, then chopped

**HAZELNUT CRUMBLE:** Make the hazelnut crumble: using the paddle attachment, in a food mixer, mix the butter and sugars until creamy. Add the vanilla extract and mix for 1 minute. Add the cinnamon, nutmeg and flour, and mix well. Add the chopped hazelnuts and mix again until everything is well combined. Remove the dough and, on a clean work surface, knead gently by hand into a ball.

Wrap the dough in cling film and place in the freezer until frozen.

Preheat the oven to 180°C fan (200°C), gas mark 6. Line a baking tray with baking paper.

Remove the dough from the freezer and leave at room temperature for 5–10 minutes to soften it a little. Coarsely grate it onto the lined baking tray, spreading it out evenly. Make sure each time you pass it through the grater, you grate it with a long continuous movement, so the crumble is as big as possible.

Bake in the preheated oven for 5–6 minutes, or until golden brown. Remove from the oven and leave to cool down at room temperature. Break it into chunky pieces by hand, if needed.

**GRANOLA:** Mix all the ingredients with the hazelnut crumble in a bowl. Transfer to an airtight container, then cover with a lid and store in a cool, dry place for up to 15 days.

For one portion, spoon the yoghurt into a shallow bowl and smooth the top. Drizzle with 1 tablespoon honey and top with the granola. Arrange the frozen blueberries, pomegranate seeds and chocolate pearls on top and drizzle with the remaining honey. Garnish with the mint. Repeat for as many portions you wish to make.

**SOUR CHERRIES & LIME TOPPING:**
200g full-fat Greek yoghurt
70g sour cherries in syrup
grated zest of ½ lime

**BERRY TOPPING:**
200g full-fat Greek yoghurt
50g strawberry jam
15 fresh blueberries
10 fresh raspberries
10 fresh blackberries
3 fresh strawberries, hulled and quartered
1 tbsp roasted pistachios, roughly chopped
6 mint tips
grated zest of ¼ lime

**GREEK YOGHURT WITH TAHINI & BANANA TOPPING:**
200g full-fat Greek yoghurt
3 tbsp thyme honey
½ banana, sliced
a small handful of walnut halves
2 tbsp tahini
¼ tsp ground cinnamon

**SOUR CHERRY TOPPING:** Spoon the yoghurt into a shallow bowl and smooth the top.

Top with the sour cherries and sprinkle with the grated lime zest.

**BERRY TOPPING:** Spoon the yoghurt into a shallow bowl and smooth the top.

Spread the strawberry jam over the yoghurt and arrange all the berries on top.

Sprinkle with pistachios in between the berries and garnish with tips of mint and lime zest.

**GREEK YOGHURT WITH TAHINI & BANANA TOPPING:** Spoon the yoghurt into a shallow bowl and smooth the top.

Spread the honey evenly over the top. Arrange the banana slices and walnuts on top, reserving a walnut half.

Drizzle with tahini and dust with the cinnamon. Using a Microplane grater, grate the reserved walnut over the top.

**NOTE:** The granola recipe makes 15 servings, but it can be stored in an airtight container in a cool, dry place for up to 15 days.

# Pancakes

To introduce the Greek brunch to London's dining scene, we had to create a signature pancake dish. All over the world, pancakes are an essential dish in any breakfast or brunch, so they could not be missing from our menus. We wanted a pancake that was thicker and fluffier and could stand on its own – in other words, a 'pan-cake'. Even without the toppings, our pan-cake is delicious, thanks to its vanilla flavour and fluffy texture. The signature pancake has been the Very Berry, but throughout the years we have added many other toppings. Here are three of our favourite ones.

MAKES 8 PANCAKES

**PANCAKE BATTER:**
- 2 medium eggs
- 480ml full-fat milk
- 1 tbsp vanilla extract with seeds
- 300g plain flour, sifted
- 4 tsp baking powder
- 1 tsp fine salt
- 2 tbsp caster sugar
- 55g unsalted butter, melted, plus extra for brushing

**VERY BERRY PANCAKE TOPPING:**
- 32 fresh blackberries
- 32 fresh raspberries
- 64 fresh blueberries
- 640g mascarpone cheese
- 240g strawberry jam
- 24 sprigs of mint
- icing sugar, for dusting

**TIP:** If you wish to bake fewer pancakes, you can keep the remaining batter in a covered container in the fridge for up to 2 days. If you don't have any silicone moulds, you can use a small pancake pan and follow the exact same baking method described.

In a large jug, mix the eggs, milk and vanilla with a hand-held electric blender or a whisk.

Mix together the flour, baking powder, salt and sugar in a bowl and then whisk into the egg mixture until you have a smooth batter. Add the melted butter and whisk again. Cover with cling film and rest overnight in the fridge.

The following day, preheat the oven to 180°C fan (200°C), gas mark 6. Place a small, shallow pan of water in the bottom of the oven to create some steam during baking.

Remove the batter from the fridge and whisk gently to refresh the mixture. Place eight round silicone moulds (7cm diameter and 3cm depth) on a tray. Brush the moulds generously with melted butter and divide the batter between them.

Place the silicone moulds in the preheated oven and bake for 17 minutes, or until puffed up and golden brown. Remove the pancakes from the moulds, remove the tray of water and bake for another 3 minutes. Set aside for a few minutes to cool down slightly before topping.

**VERY BERRY PANCAKE TOPPING:** Freeze the berries – this will add a refreshing texture to the final dish.

Place a pancake in the middle of a plate. Spoon 80g of mascarpone cheese on top, hollowing it to create a nest and fill with 30g strawberry jam. Arrange four frozen blackberries and four frozen raspberries alternately on the edge of the mascarpone and place eight blueberries in the centre on top of the jam. Garnish with three sprigs of mint and dust with icing sugar. Serve immediately. Repeat for the remaining seven pancakes.

**LOTUS SAUCE:**

140ml full-fat milk

140g Lotus Biscoff Smooth Spread

**LOTUS CRUMBLE:**

200g milk chocolate (40% cocoa solids), melted

80g Lotus Biscoff Smooth Spread

a pinch of sea salt flakes

40g Lotus Biscoff biscuits, roughly crumbled

**GARNISH:**

480g milk chocolate cream (*see page 272*)

4 bananas, halved and sliced

8 Lotus Biscoff biscuits, roughly broken

4 tbsp chocolate pearls

**LOTUS TOPPING:** Make the Lotus sauce: gently warm the milk in a saucepan set over a medium heat until the temperature is 70°C (use a sugar thermometer to measure this). Remove the pan from the heat and mix in the Lotus spread with a whisk. Strain the sauce into a squeezy bottle and keep in the fridge.

Make the Lotus crumble: using a rubber spatula, mix the melted chocolate, Lotus spread and sea salt in a bowl. Add the crumbled biscuits and fold in gently to distribute them evenly throughout the mixture.

Spread the mixture out in a 5mm-thick layer on a tray lined with baking paper and leave in the freezer until frozen. Remove and cut into 5mm square cubes, then return to the freezer.

Place a baked pancake in the middle of a serving plate. Pipe 60g of the milk chocolate cream around the top edge of the pancake and fill the centre with ½ sliced banana. Drizzle with 35g Lotus sauce. Top with a broken Lotus biscuit, ½ tablespoon chocolate pearls and 40g Lotus crumble and serve. Repeat for the remaining seven pancakes.

**PEANUT BUTTER CHOCOLATE CRUMBLE:**

160g milk chocolate (40% cocoa solids), melted

160g crunchy peanut butter

**GARNISH:**

480g milk chocolate cream (*see page 277*)

16 tbsp salted caramel sauce (*see page 277*)

80g roasted salted peanuts

240g crunchy peanut butter

**PEANUT BUTTER CHOCOLATE CRUMBLE TOPPING:** Make the peanut butter chocolate crumble: put the melted chocolate and peanut butter in a bowl and mix with a spatula or wooden spoon until well combined.

Spread the mixture in a 5mm-thick layer on a tray lined with baking paper and place in the freezer. When frozen, cut into 5mm square cubes and return to the freezer until required.

Place a baked pancake in the middle of a serving plate. Pipe 60g milk chocolate cream around the top edge to create a small nest. Fill the nest with 1 tablespoon salted caramel sauce, then top with 10g roasted peanuts, 30g peanut butter and 40g peanut butter chocolate crumble. Drizzle another tablespoon of salted caramel over the top and serve. Repeat for the remaining seven pancakes.

# Greek Toast

Inspired by the ubiquitous and much-loved French toast, we came up with a special brioche recipe, made with tahini to give it a Greek twist, and we named it Greek toast. We wanted to create some special toppings that incorporate familiar flavours, especially ones that were rooted in our childhood. The apple crumble topping comes from the aroma of a freshly baked apple pie, which woke us up at weekends. The fragrance of the baked crumbly pastry combined with the sweetness and sourness of the warm apples was extraordinary and the inspiration for our first topping for Greek toast. Our other favourite topping is an irresistible peanut and banana combo topped with salted caramel ice cream.

**SERVES 1**

70g slice brioche loaf, approx. 3cm thick (*see page 214*)
20g caster sugar

**CRÈME ANGLAISE:**
15g caster sugar
3 medium egg yolks
200ml full-fat milk
150ml single cream
(Note: This is enough for 10 brioche slices)

Make the crème anglaise: in a bowl, whisk the sugar and egg yolks until well combined.

Heat the milk and cream in a saucepan set over a low to medium heat to 50°C (use a sugar thermometer to measure the temperature). Pour over the egg yolk mixture, whisk to incorporate and then return to the pan. Heat gently over a low to medium heat, stirring constantly with a rubber spatula and scraping the bottom of the pan, until the temperature reaches 82°C. Strain immediately through a sieve into a bowl and place some cling film on the surface of the mixture to prevent a skin forming. Leave to cool in the fridge.

Dip the brioche slice briefly into the cold crème anglaise to cover it on both sides, then drain on kitchen paper. Sprinkle a thin layer of sugar on each side and caramelize with a blow torch. Repeat with another thin layer of sugar on each side to create a crisp finish.

Top the Greek toast with one of the toppings below.

Tip: Don't be tempted to skip the second caramelizing process – it makes the Greek toast crisper and even more delicious.

**APPLE CRUMBLE GREEK TOAST:**

15g unsalted butter
25g soft light brown sugar
1 apple, peeled, cored and cut into 1.5cm cubes
1 tsp vanilla extract with seeds
a pinch of ground cinnamon
a pinch of fine salt
15g hazelnut crumble (*see page 276*)
1 scoop vanilla ice cream
1 tbsp salted caramel sauce (*see page 277*)

**PEANUT BUTTER & BANANA GREEK TOAST:**

½ banana, thickly sliced
3 tbsp smooth peanut butter, in a piping bag
½ tbsp dark chocolate pearls
1 scoop salted caramel ice cream

**CARAMELIZED HAZELNUTS:**

30g unsalted roasted hazelnuts
80ml simple syrup (*see page 276*)
sunflower oil, for deep-frying

**APPLE CRUMBLE GREEK TOAST:** Melt the butter in a saucepan set over a medium heat. Stir in the sugar and mix to combine.

Add the apple, then stir in the vanilla extract, cinnamon and salt and cook gently, stirring occasionally, for 5 minutes, or until the apple caramelizes.

Place the caramelized apple on top of the Greek toast and sprinkle with two-thirds of the hazelnut crumble.

Add the ice cream, drizzle with salted caramel sauce and sprinkle the remaining hazelnut streusel over the top.

**PEANUT BUTTER & BANANA GREEK TOAST:** Make the caramelized hazelnuts: put the hazelnuts and syrup in a saucepan set over a low heat and simmer gently until the syrup caramelizes and starts to get sticky.

Strain the hazelnuts and immediately fry them in a heavy-based saucepan of sunflower oil at 180°C for 2–3 minutes, or until golden brown. Remove with a slotted spoon, drain on kitchen paper and set aside to cool.

When they are cool, place in a zipper bag and crush them roughly with a rolling pin.

Arrange the sliced banana on top of the Greek toast. Pipe the peanut butter on top of the banana and add half of the chocolate pearls. Add the ice cream and sprinkle with the caramelized hazelnuts and the remaining chocolate pearls.

# Rizogalo Brûlée

The name *rizogalo* comes from the Greek words *rizi* (rice) and *gala* (milk). A popular dessert in Greece, it is served warm or chilled, and is loved for its simplicity, delightful texture and perfect pairing with cinnamon. Like many other simple dishes, it is cherished and has been passed down through generations and enjoyed by people of all ages. In our version, we coat the traditional *rizogalo* with a thin layer of sugar and then caramelize it.

**SERVES 4**

90g arborio rice (dry weight)
800ml water
1 medium egg
3 medium egg yolks
40g cornflour
350ml full-fat milk
150ml single cream
70g caster sugar
1 vanilla pod, plus scraped-out seeds
40g unsalted butter, cubed

**TO SERVE:**
caster sugar, for sprinkling
a handful of fresh raspberries
a handful of fresh blackberries
a handful of fresh blueberries
icing sugar, for dusting
ground cinnamon, for dusting

Add the rice and water in a saucepan set over a high heat. Bring to the boil, then reduce to a simmer and cook for 15 minutes, or until the rice is tender but al dente. Strain and spread the rice out on a tray to cool down. Cover with baking paper, attached to the surface of the rice to prevent a crust forming.

In a bowl, whisk the egg, egg yolks and cornflour until well combined.

Warm the milk, cream, sugar, scraped-out vanilla pod and seeds in a saucepan set over a low to medium heat and whisk gently to dissolve the sugar. Strain through a sieve into the egg mixture, whisk to combine and return the mixture back to the pan.

Cook gently over a medium heat, whisking constantly, until the cornflour activates and the mixture starts to thicken. Reduce the heat to low and cook gently to cook out the starchy flavour of the cornflour, whisking constantly for 3 minutes. Remove from the heat, stir in the butter and then stir in the rice.

Divide the mixture between four serving bowls and flatten the surface. Leave in the fridge until cold and set.

Once set, remove from the fridge and sprinkle a thin layer of sugar over the top. Caramelize with a blowtorch, then place the berries on one side of each bowl and dust them with icing sugar and cinnamon. Serve immediately.

# EGGS

Rich yolks and delicate whites are the focus of the modern Greek brunch, and the foundations for many of our dishes. Whether it's simple sunny-side-up eggs with feta cheese or indulgent eggs Benedict with Greek yoghurt hollandaise, eggs are the versatile stars of this modern meal. At the heart of it all is an appreciation for high-quality produce sourced from the fertile soil of Greece. Picture free-range eggs with deeply orange yolks served sunny-side-up and cooked with foraged greens and browned butter, or runny poached eggs simmered in a sweet, smoked tomato sauce, topped with spicy green peppers and chilli. Fresh vegetables, fragrant herbs, succulent meats and artisanal cheeses have become the egg's perfect companions.
Enjoyed al fresco on a sun-dappled Greek terrace or inside on a rainy day in London, the modern Greek brunch is an invitation to gather with friends and family, to slow down and savour the moment. Nothing beats lingering over good food and revelling in an abundance of traditional Greek flavours, served with a quirky twist.

*'Will Greek Sundays ever change? I hope not! I cherish lazy Sundays spent lounging with my kids before planning an impromptu late lunch with family and friends. There's nothing better than gathering at a taverna around a table where the humble Greek salad, tzatziki and charcoaled meats and fish are the star attractions. This is how we, the new generation of Greeks, were raised, and it is truly remarkable. Would I add something to these special Sunday meals? Yes! Every now and then I would enjoy a well-cooked modern Greek brunch, which is inspired by the simplicity of the good old Greek breakfast!'*
**NIKOS**

# Village Eggs

Greece is famous for its spectacular coastline and islands but it offers much more than stunning beaches and clear blue water. It has a diverse and unique landscape with snow-capped mountains, dense forests, fast-flowing rivers, lakes and waterfalls. Nestled in the mountains are small villages, each one with its own remarkable culinary history. The villagers utilize local, sustainable foods, such as horta, which are foraged seasonal varieties of leafy 'wild mountain greens'. The locals often pair them with free-range eggs from their backyards, creating a unique and delicious combination of flavours.

**SERVES 1**

120g foraged greens or market greens (e.g. chard), washed
2 tbsp extra-virgin olive oil, plus extra for frying the egg
½ tsp lemon juice, strained
a pinch of fine salt
1 large free-range egg
20g goat's curd cheese, cut into pieces
grated zest of ¼ lemon
a pinch of sea salt flakes
2 twists of freshly ground Madagascar pepper
2 chives, finely chopped
2 slices sourdough bread (*see page 202*), toasted

**SMOKED YOGHURT:**

2 spring onions, trimmed and peeled
2 tsp extra-virgin olive oil
¼ garlic clove, grated (with a Microplane grater)
a pinch of sea salt flakes
2 twists of freshly ground white pepper
100g full-fat Greek yoghurt

Make the smoked yoghurt: chargrill the spring onions over charcoal until blackened. Alternatively, bake in a preheated oven at 180°C fan (200°C), gas mark 6 for 40 minutes, or until blackened and crispy.

Chop the charred spring onions and pulse in a blender until powdery.

Transfer the spring onion powder to a bowl and mix with the olive oil, garlic, salt and pepper, and yoghurt until well combined. Set aside.

Blanch the greens in a pan of boiling water for 2–4 minutes, or until just tender. Drain and then plunge into a bowl of iced water to cool down. Remove and pat dry with kitchen paper.

Place them in a bowl and sprinkle with 1 tablespoon olive oil. Chargrill them over charcoal or in a grill pan, tossing them for 2 minutes, or until just charred. Return to the bowl and add the remaining olive oil, lemon juice and salt.

Fry the egg, sunny-side up, in some olive oil in a frying pan until the white is cooked but the yolk is still runny.

Spread the smoked yoghurt in the centre of a rustic earthenware bowl and arrange the greens on top. Place the fried egg in the middle and scatter the goat's curd cheese around it. Season with the lemon zest, salt and pepper and sprinkle the chives over the egg yolk. Serve with toasted sourdough bread.

**TIP:** If you can't find goat's curd cheese, use feta or any good-quality soft goat's cheese instead.

# Greek Eggs Benedict & Royale

Both classic eggs Benedict and eggs Royale feature poached eggs on English muffins topped with hollandaise sauce. Benedict is served with bacon, and royale with smoked salmon. We wanted to include them in our brunch, which presented us with a challenge: how to create something new with a modern Greek touch while paying homage to the original dishes. The breakthrough came with our version of the hollandaise sauce. Traditional hollandaise is made with yolks, fat (clarified butter) and acid (vinegar), cooked over a bain-marie. Mayonnaise is essentially a cold version of hollandaise using a different fat (typically sunflower oil). We enriched our garlic mayonnaise with Greek yoghurt to make a cold 'hollandaise sauce'. The yoghurt introduces a pleasant acidity, making the sauce rounder. We also replaced the muffin with koulouri milk bread to create a dish that retains the familiar flavours of classic eggs Benedict while incorporating inventive Greek elements.

SERVES 1

### GREEK EGGS BENEDICT:

800ml water
100ml red or white wine vinegar
1 large free-range egg
1 tbsp extra-virgin olive oil, plus extra for drizzling
100g pancetta, finely diced
100g red onion, finely diced
1 koulouri bread (*see page 198*)
5 flat-leaf parsley leaves, thinly sliced

### GREEK YOGHURT HOLLANDAISE:

40g garlic mayo (*see page 270*)
¼ tsp sherry vinegar
1 tbsp full-fat Greek yoghurt
a pinch of fine salt

### GREEK EGGS BENEDICT

Make the Greek yoghurt hollandaise: whisk all the ingredients together until well combined. Cover and keep in the fridge until you're ready to serve.

Poach the egg: half-fill a saucepan with the water and vinegar and set over a low to medium heat. When it starts to simmer, carefully crack the egg and slide it into the water. Cook for 5–6 minutes, or until the white is cooked through.

With a slotted spoon, carefully transfer the egg to a shallow pan of hot water to remove the vinegar taste and keep it warm.

While the egg is cooking, heat the olive oil in a frying pan set over a medium heat. Add the pancetta and onion and cook for 10 minutes, or until the onion is tender and translucent and the bacon is golden brown and crisp. Remove and drain on kitchen paper.

Place the koulouri in the centre of a serving plate. Carefully remove the poached egg from the warm water and drain on kitchen paper, then place it gently in the middle of the koulouri. Cover with the Greek yoghurt hollandaise and top with the pancetta and onion. Drizzle with olive oil, sprinkle with parsley and serve immediately.

**GREEK EGGS ROYALE:**

800ml water

100ml red or white wine vinegar

1 large free-range egg

40g kale, washed and roughly chopped

1 tbsp extra-virgin olive oil

a pinch of fine salt

½ tsp lemon juice, strained

1 koulouri bread (*see page 198*)

1 quantity Greek yoghurt hollandaise (*see page 174*)

120g smoked salmon, thinly sliced

3g fresh horseradish

1 tbsp trout or salmon roe

**GREEK EGGS ROYALE**

Poach the egg (see steps 2–3 in the recipe page 174).

Blanch the kale in a pan of boiling water for 2 minutes. Drain and then plunge into a bowl of iced water to cool down. Remove and pat dry with kitchen paper.

Transfer the kale to a bowl, sprinkle with olive oil and season with salt. Grill over charcoal or in a cast iron skillet set over a high heat until just starting to char. Return to the bowl and stir in the lemon juice.

Place the koulouri bread in the centre of a serving plate and put the poached egg in the middle of the koulouri. Top with the Greek yoghurt hollandaise plus the charred kale and smoked salmon. Using a Microplane grater, grate the horseradish over the top and garnish with a spoonful of trout roe.

# Green Kayanas

*Kayanas* is a simple and speedy dish made with tomatoes and eggs. It was our childhood go-to meal when our parents were late home from work. We never complained if it was their 15 minute dinner solution as we loved it so much. The preparation is straightforward: coarsely grate some tomatoes and whisk a few eggs as if you're making an omelette – the tomato to egg ratio should be 2:1. Lightly cook the tomatoes in a pan, stir in the beaten eggs and cook quickly, then remove from the heat and add feta. In our version of kayanas we cook tomatoes and eggs separately and along with the feta cheese we add a spicy avocado mash.

**SERVES 1**

2 large free-range eggs
20ml full-fat milk
a pinch of fine salt
20g unsalted butter
4 confit cherry tomatoes (*see page 271*), halved
20g barrel-matured feta cheese, cut into pieces
a pinch of dried oregano
extra-virgin olive oil, for drizzling
2 slices sourdough bread (*see page 202*), toasted

**AVOCADO MASH:**

1 small avocado, peeled and stoned
2 tsp lime juice, strained
3–4 drops Tabasco, according to taste
½ small tomato, skinned, deseeded and chopped
a pinch of fine salt
¼ garlic clove, finely chopped
a small handful of coriander leaves, chopped

Make the avocado mash: place the avocado flesh in a bowl and smash it with a fork. Add the remaining ingredients and mix well. For a smooth purée, blend with a hand-held electric blender. Place some cling film on the surface and chill in the fridge until you're ready to serve.

Whisk the eggs, milk and salt in a bowl. Heat the butter in a frying pan set over a medium heat and add the egg mixture. Cook, folding constantly with a rubber spatula, until scrambled and creamy.

Plate half of the avocado mash in the centre of a serving plate. Place the scrambled eggs on top, hiding the avocado. Top the scrambled eggs with the remaining avocado mash and arrange the confit cherry tomatoes and feta on top. Sprinkle with the dried oregano and drizzle with olive oil. Serve with toasted sourdough bread.

# Mountain Eggs

The Zagorohoria region in north-western Greece is a must-visit destination if you want to experience the stunning beauty of its mountains. We enjoyed exploring its scenic villages and charming family-owned tavernas and discovered that the locals take great pride in the gastronomic gems from their forests. The region is renowned for its delicious mushrooms, which are a staple in the local diet. Our culinary journeys through this remarkable region inspired us to create new recipes, especially with mushrooms and truffles, and this dish is our homage to the great times we spent there and the amazing food.

*'A man of great respect, a good friend, food lover and a true bon viveur, introduced me to the Zagorohoria region for the first time, sharing his love for its culinary treasures.'* **NIKOS**

### SERVES 1

2 large free-range eggs
20ml full-fat milk
a pinch of fine salt
20g butter, unsalted
5g fresh black truffle, thinly sliced
2–3 chives, finely chopped
extra-virgin olive oil, for drizzling
2 slices sourdough bread (see page 202), toasted

**MUSHROOM PURÉE:**

2 tbsp extra-virgin olive oil
½ small red onion, diced
150g button mushrooms, peeled, stemmed and thinly sliced
a pinch of fine salt
1 tsp ruby red port
2 tsp single cream
20g unsalted butter
a twist of freshly ground white pepper

**SHIITAKE MUSHROOMS:**

1 tbsp extra-virgin olive oil
1 ½ tbsp finely diced red onion
¼ garlic clove, finely chopped
100g shiitake mushrooms, cleaned, stemmed and roughly chopped
1 thyme sprig
20g unsalted butter

Make the mushroom purée: heat the olive oil in a shallow pan set over a low to medium heat. Add the onion and cook for 4–5 minutes, or until tender. Add the mushrooms and salt, then cover the pan with a lid to create some steam. Cook for 5–10 minutes, or until the mushrooms have softened and all the juices have evaporated. Add the port and cook for 1 minute, or until all the alcohol has evaporated, disguard any remaining liquid.

Transfer the mushrooms to a blender and add the cream, butter and pepper. Blend to a smooth purée, then transfer to a bowl, cover and keep warm.

Cook the shiitake mushrooms: heat the olive oil in a pan set over a medium heat and sauté the onion for 4–5 minutes, or until translucent. Add the garlic and cook for 1 minute. Add the mushrooms and thyme and sauté until the mushrooms are cooked through and golden. Take the pan off the heat and stir in the butter. Set aside.

Whisk the eggs, milk and salt together in a bowl.

Heat the butter in a small saucepan set over a medium heat and add the egg mixture. Cook, stirring constantly with a rubber spatula, until the eggs are creamy and starting to scramble.

Put the mushroom purée in the middle of a serving dish and cover with the scrambled eggs (they should hide the mushroom purée underneath). Top with the cooked shiitake mushrooms and freshly shave the black truffle over them. Sprinkle with chives and drizzle with olive oil. Serve immediately with toasted sourdough bread.

# Open Pitta Lamb

Throughout our cooking tests and trials, we have experimented with stuffing pretty much every ingredient inside a pitta flatbread. From meats and fish with sauces to fresh salads and cooked vegetables, we've tried them all. However, we wanted to create a brunch dish with a more refined appearance, and this was the impetus for the open pitta. Inspired by the open sandwich, after numerous trials, we ended up with what became one of our brunch signature dishes: the open pitta lamb.

**SERVES 1**

180g lamb rump cap (or roasted lamb shoulder)
a pinch of fine salt
½ tbsp extra-virgin olive oil, plus extra for the egg and pitta
a pinch of sea salt flakes
1 large free-range egg
1 large pitta flatbread, 14cm diameter (see page 212)
80g smoked tomato sauce (see page 268)
a pinch of sweet and smoked paprika
2 twists of freshly ground Madagascar pepper
3–4 chives, thinly chopped

**CUMIN YOGHURT:**

40g full-fat Greek yoghurt
a pinch of ground cumin
a pinch of chilli powder
a pinch of ground cloves
a pinch of fine salt
1 tsp extra-virgin olive oil
¼ garlic clove, grated with a Microplane grater

Make the cumin yoghurt: mix all ingredients together in a bowl. Cover and keep in the fridge until you're ready to serve.

Preheat the oven to 180°C fan (200°C), gas mark 6.

Season the lamb with the fine salt. Heat the olive oil in an ovenproof frying pan set over a medium heat and quickly sear the lamb on all sides. Transfer to the preheated oven and cook for 10–15 minutes, or until medium. Remove from the oven and rest for 5 minutes before cutting into 5mm-thick slices. Season with sea salt flakes.

Fry the egg, sunny-side up, in some olive oil in a frying pan until the white is cooked but the yolk is still runny.

Drizzle the pitta flatbread with a few drops of olive oil and grill or toast until crisp on the outside and fluffy inside. Cut into eight triangles, pizza-style, and arrange them in the middle of a serving plate.

Spread the cumin yoghurt over the pitta triangles and then spread with the smoked tomato sauce. Cover with the lamb slices and place the fried egg on top. Dust with paprika, season with pepper and sprinkle with chopped chives.

# Eggs Saganaki

Tomatoes and feta are a staple combo in Greek cuisine and feature in many traditional hot and cold dishes. The classic cold dish is the Greek salad (horiatiki), whereas saganaki is a popular hot one. The term saganaki refers to the cooking technique named after a shallow pan widely used for stove-top cooking. It typically involves ingredients, such as prawns, sausages and vegetables, simmered in a fragrant tomato sauce and finished with feta. And because tomatoes and feta pair so well with eggs, we created our own eggs saganaki – the ultimate comfort food. This could easily become a signature dish for your home brunch.

**SERVES 2**

800ml water
100ml red or white wine vinegar
2 large free-range eggs
100g spinach, washed and chopped
2 tbsp extra-virgin olive oil
2 pinches of sea salt flakes
1 tsp lemon juice, strained
6 Padron peppers
2 spring onions, chopped
240g smoked tomato sauce (see page 268)
4 confit pearl onions (see page 271)
30g barrel-matured feta cheese, cut into 8 pieces
a pinch of sweet and smoked paprika
a twist of freshly ground Madagascar pepper
2 slices sourdough bread (see page 202), toasted

Preheat the oven to 180°C fan (200°C), gas mark 6.

Poach the eggs: half-fill a large saucepan with the water and vinegar and set over a low to medium heat. When it starts to simmer, carefully crack the eggs and slide them into the water at a distance from each other. Cook for 5–6 minutes, or until the whites are cooked through.

With a slotted spoon, carefully transfer the eggs to a shallow pan filled with hot water to remove the vinegar taste and keep them warm.

In a pan set over a medium heat, sauté the spinach in 1 tablespoon olive oil until lightly wilted, then transfer to a bowl and season with a pinch of sea salt and ½ teaspoon lemon juice. In the same pan, sauté the peppers and spring onions in the remaining 1 tablespoon olive oil until lightly coloured. Transfer to another bowl and season with a pinch of sea salt and the remaining ½ teaspoon lemon juice.

Place the spinach in an ovenproof dish and cover with the smoked tomato sauce, leaving some spinach visible in places. With a spoon, make two small 'nests' in the smoked tomato sauce. Remove the poached eggs from the warm water and drain on kitchen paper, then place them gently in the nests. Arrange the Padron peppers, spring onions, confit pearl onions and feta on top.

Cover with a lid and bake in the preheated oven for 6 minutes. Remove and season with paprika and Madagascar pepper. Serve with toasted sourdough bread on the side.

# BOWLS

In the fast-paced world of modern dining, bowls have emerged as an adaptable and nourishing option for anyone seeking a satisfying and healthy meal. In the realm of the modern Greek brunch, bowls take centre stage, carefully crafted to balance bold flavours with nutritional needs.

We use ancient grains and legumes, vibrant greens, seasonal vegetables, pasta and succulent meat and fish to create our modern Greek brunch bowls. They offer a feast for the senses, which is as satisfying as it is delicious. They are a new addition to our repertoire and already it's hard to imagine the concept of the modern Greek brunch without them. These bowls are a way to start the day and can be prepared quickly. And, what's more, they're a healthy option, offering a balanced mix of carbs, vegetables and protein.

# Spicy Chicken Bowl

This comforting bowl combines chargrilled chicken with pasta, and to enhance the delicious smoky flavour and crunchiness, we have grilled the cooked pasta in a special perforated pan over charcoal. The soya-based sauce is reduced to a caramel consistency to add a sweet and savoury taste while the spiciness comes from a homemade chilli crunch. Finally, the avocado brings a buttery texture, wrapping up all the flavours together in a single dish.

**SERVES 1**

40g canned sweetcorn kernels, drained
1 tsp chilli crunch (see page 273)
1 x 200g boned chicken thigh
1 tsp spice rub (see page 275)
½ avocado, peeled, stoned and sliced
sea salt flakes, for seasoning
freshly ground Madagascar pepper, for seasoning
½ tsp extra-virgin olive oil
½ tsp lemon juice
1 large free-range egg, soft-boiled for 7–8 minutes
1 tbsp soya caramel (see page 275)

**PASTA:**
100g fusilli pasta (dry weight)
1 tbsp extra-virgin olive oil
50g unsalted butter
1 tsp lemon juice, strained
a generous pinch of sea salt flakes
2–3 twists of freshly ground Madagascar pepper

In a bowl, mix the sweetcorn with ½ teaspoon chilli crunch, then set aside.

Coat the chicken thigh all over with the spice rub. Chargrill over hot coals on a barbecue, turning occasionally, for 12–15 minutes, or until cooked through. Remove from the heat and cut the chicken into 1cm-thick slices.

Meanwhile, cook the pasta: add to a saucepan of boiling water and cook (according to the instructions on the packet) until al dente. Drain in a colander, then drizzle with olive oil.

Transfer the pasta to a perforated pan and chargrill on the barbecue, tossing occasionally, for 3–4 minutes.

Meanwhile, melt the butter in a pan set over a medium heat and cook gently, swirling the pan, until it turns light brown in colour. Add the pasta and toss in the butter. Transfer to a bowl, stir in the lemon juice and season with sea salt and pepper.

Transfer the pasta to a serving bowl and arrange the sliced chicken on one side, and a fan of sliced avocado and the sweetcorn on the other. Season the avocado slices with a pinch of sea salt flakes, a twist of pepper, the olive oil and the lemon juice.

Peel the soft-boiled egg, cut in half and place in the middle of the bowl. Season the egg with a pinch of sea salt flakes and a twist of pepper.

Glaze the sliced chicken with the soya caramel and sprinkle the remaining ½ teaspoon chilli crunch on top. Serve immediately.

# Tuna Bowl

In recent years, the traditional Hawaiian poke bowl has become globally popular. It typically features diced raw fish served on a base of cooked rice and can be modified easily by adding a variety of toppings. We have created our own Greek version using trahanas pasta instead of rice. This lovely bowl is rich in protein, vegetables and carbs, making it a nutritious option that can be enjoyed at any time of the day.

**SERVES 1**

- 100g trahanas pasta, sweet (dry weight)
- 5 tsp extra-virgin olive oil
- 1 tbsp chimichurri (*see page 272*)
- a small handful of mint leaves, thinly sliced
- 3 tsp lemon juice, strained
- a generous pinch of fine salt
- 3–4 twists of freshly ground Madagascar pepper
- 80g flat green beans
- a pinch of sea salt flakes
- 180g yellowfin tuna loin
- 150g shimeji mushrooms

Cook the trahanas in a saucepan of boiling water for 5 minutes. Drain and rinse under cold running water to cool down. Drain again and transfer to a bowl. Mix with 2 teaspoons olive oil to prevent the grains sticking to each other, then cover and place in the fridge for 10 minutes to cool.

Remove the trahanas from the fridge and add the chimichurri, mint and 2 teaspoons lemon juice. Season with fine salt and pepper, then mix gently and set aside.

Blanch the green beans in a saucepan of boiling water for 4 minutes, then plunge into a bowl of iced water. Drain and pat dry with kitchen paper. Heat 1 teaspoon olive oil in a pan set over a medium heat, add the green beans and sauté for 2 minutes, or until slightly coloured. Remove from the pan and cut into thin strips. Transfer to a bowl and season with sea salt flakes and the remaining 1 teaspoon lemon juice.

Brush the tuna all over with 1 teaspoon olive oil. Sear it quickly on all sides in a pan set over a high heat. Do not overcook – it should be just seared on the outside and rare inside. Remove from the pan and place on a plate. Cover and leave in the fridge to cool before cutting into 1cm-thick slices.

Meanwhile, preheat the oven to 180°C fan (200°C), gas mark 6. Drizzle the mushrooms with the remaining 1 teaspoon olive oil and bake in the preheated oven for 10 minutes, or until cooked through.

Arrange the trahanas pasta in a serving bowl and fan the tuna slices on one side, and the green beans on the other. Place the mushrooms in the middle and serve immediately.

**TIP**: You can use thick bulgur or barley for this recipe if you cannot find any trahanas pasta.

# Kale & Feta Bowl

Kale is a versatile and hardy leafy green that is grown in both spring and autumn. We often use it in salads as well as comforting brunch dishes. The recipe for this bowl is simple in the making but packed with flavours for such a light and healthy dish.

SERVES 1

120g kale, washed and roughly chopped
2 tsp extra-virgin olive oil, plus extra for drizzling
a pinch of fine salt
1 tsp lemon juice, strained
10 cherry tomatoes, quartered
1 large free-range egg, soft-boiled for 7–8 minutes
½ avocado, peeled and stoned
20g feta cheese, crumbled
a pinch of sea salt flakes
2 twists of freshly ground Madagascar pepper

**TOMATO & CORIANDER SALSA:**

2 tomatoes
½ red onion, finely diced
5 tbsp extra-virgin olive oil
½ tbsp lime juice, strained
a small handful of coriander leaves, thinly sliced
a pinch of fine salt
a few drops of Tabasco

Make the tomato and coriander salsa: cut a cross in the bottom of the tomatoes and blanch in a saucepan of boiling water for 8 seconds. Remove and plunge into a bowl of ice.

Peel the tomatoes and cut into wedges. Remove the seeds and pat dry the tomato flesh with kitchen paper. Cut the flesh into small dice and transfer to a bowl. Add the remaining ingredients and mix gently. Place in the fridge until ready to serve.

Blanch the kale for 2 minutes in a saucepan of boiling water and then plunge into a bowl of iced water. Drain and pat dry with kitchen paper. Transfer to a bowl and toss gently with the olive oil and fine salt. Chargrill the kale, turning occasionally, in a cast iron skillet set over a high heat for 2 minutes. Remove and return to the bowl, then toss in the lemon juice. Add the cherry tomatoes and mix gently.

Peel the soft-boiled egg and cut in half.

Cut the avocado into 5mm-thick slices.

Put the kale and tomatoes in a serving bowl. Drizzle with the tomato and coriander salsa. Arrange the avocado slices on one side. Crumble the feta cheese over the other side and place the egg halves in the middle and lightly season the eggs and avocado with sea salt flakes and pepper. Drizzle with olive oil and serve immediately.

198 Koulouri Bread
202 Village Sourdough
206 Vasilopita (New Year Cake)
208 Tahini Brioche
212 Cinnamon Rolls
214 Pitta Flatbreads
216 Tsoureki

# Baking

# MAKING BREAD

Bread holds a special place on every Greek table. The aroma of freshly baked bread wafting through the air is a familiar and comforting scent in Greek households, evoking memories of family meals and celebrations. It's an essential staple in every home, bringing warmth and tradition to each meal. Baking is deeply revered in our country's culinary traditions and remains a cornerstone of Greek cuisine and culture. From ancient times right up to the present, bread has symbolized nourishment, hospitality and community. Throughout history, the act of baking bread has been intertwined with rituals, traditions and communal gatherings.

Beyond its culinary and cultural importance, bread also holds symbolic significance in Greek society. In the Greek Orthodox tradition, it plays a central role in religious rituals and ceremonies, symbolizing the body of Christ and representing the communal bond among the faithful. During religious holidays and celebrations, special breads, such as prosfora, are baked and offered as part of the Eucharistic liturgy, reinforcing the sacred connection between food, faith and community. Tsoureki, a plaited sweet bread flavoured with mastiha and mahleb, is a necessity for our Easter celebrations, a symbol of the resurrection and new life.

Baking bread at home is a time-honoured tradition in Greece, passed down through generations and steeped in familial knowledge and expertise. Many Greek families take pride in their ability to bake using traditional methods and family recipes. From kneading the dough to shaping the loaves and baking them in a wood-fired oven or a modern electric one, the process of making bread is a rewarding labour of love that requires skill, patience and attention to detail.

*'We have grown up with bread being an essential part of our daily lives, and it holds a special place in our hearts. A substantial meal, capable of sustaining us throughout the day, is bread accompanied by shapeless pieces of feta or aged firm kasseri cheese (made from cow's milk), a handful of olives and a juicy ripe tomato drizzled with extra virgin olive oil.'*

**ANDREAS**

# Koulouri bread

One of the most iconic breads originating from Thessaloniki, Greece's second-largest city, is koulouri. It used to be the king of street foods and was served simply and modestly with a piece of *kasseri* yellow cheese. The sellers filled their big wooden trays with a pile of *koulouria* and put them on top of their heads to walk around the city until they sold out. Today you can still find street sellers, but they use wheeled carts instead. Alongside koulouria, they often offer delicious Greek doughnuts dusted in caster sugar, called loukoumades.

**MAKES 10 KOULOURIA**

220ml water
75g unsalted butter, cubed
40g caster sugar
25g milk powder
425g strong white bread flour (T55), sifted
10g fine salt
6g fast-action dried yeast
100g sesame seeds

Put the water, butter, sugar and milk powder in a saucepan set over a low heat and whisk gently until dissolved. Strain through a fine sieve into a bowl and leave to cool in the fridge.

In a food mixer bowl, whisk by hand the flour, salt and yeast until well combined. Then attach the bowl to the mixer, fitted with the dough hook attachment. With the motor running, slowly add the cold milk powder mixture, a little at a time, mixing until well combined. Continue mixing for 15 minutes, or until an elastic and silky dough is formed.

Transfer the dough to a bowl and cover with cling film. Leave to rest in the fridge for 30 minutes. You can use it the same day or following day.

Remove from the fridge and place the dough on a clean work surface. Fold it over once or twice to refresh it and then cut it into ten equal-sized portions (70g each) and shape each one into a ball. Knead with your hands and, using your palms, roll out each portion into a long cylindrical shape, approximately 20cm long and 2cm thick. Bring the edges together, overlapping them, to form a ring. Pinch them and, using two fingers, roll them together to make the connection invisible. Stretch the dough ring gently until you have a 4cm-wide hole in the middle of each koulouri.

Place the sesame seeds in a bowl. Pour some water into another bowl and add some ice cubes to make an ice bath. Quickly immerse the shaped koulouria, one by one, in the ice bath and immediately dip them into the sesame seeds, swirling the bowl to coat them all over. Place on a baking tray lined with baking paper.

Use your oven as a proofer by placing a shallow pan of water at the bottom and preheating it to 50°C, or the lowest temperature possible for gas (leaving the gas oven door slightly open). Place the koulouria in the oven and proof for 45 minutes.

Remove from the oven and increase the temperature to 180°C fan (200°C), gas mark 6. Leave the pan of water in the oven.

Bake the koulouri in the preheated oven for 10 minutes, then remove the pan of water and bake for a further 12–15 minutes, or until golden brown. Remove from the oven and leave on the baking tray to cool at room temperature. These are best eaten the same day.

**TIP**: You can also use this dough recipe to make hot dog buns, see below.

MAKES 10 HOT DOG BUNS

**HOT DOG BUN**

Follow the Koulouri Bread recipe until step 3.

Remove from the fridge and place the dough on a clean work surface. Fold it over once or twice to refresh it and then cut it into ten equal-sized portions (70g each) and shape each one into a ball. Knead with your hands and, using your palms, roll out each portion into a mini oval-baguette shape, approximately 12cm long and 4cm thick. Place them in a baguette baking tray, spacing them 8cm apart, or on a normal baking tray both lined with baking paper.

Use your oven as a proofer by placing a shallow pan of water at the bottom and preheating it to 50°C, or the lowest temperature possible for gas (leaving the gas oven door slightly open). Place the tray in the oven and proof for 45 minutes.

Meanwhile, make the craquelin from the village sourdough recipe (*see page 202*).

Remove the tray from the oven and increase the temperature to 180°C fan (200°C), gas mark 6. Leave the pan of water in the oven.

Gently spread 2 tablespoons of the cold craquelin mixture on top of every proofed bun. Bake the buns in the preheated oven for 10 minutes, then remove the pan of water and bake for a further 12–15 minutes until golden brown. Remove from the oven and leave on the tray to cool at room temperature. Use the same day.

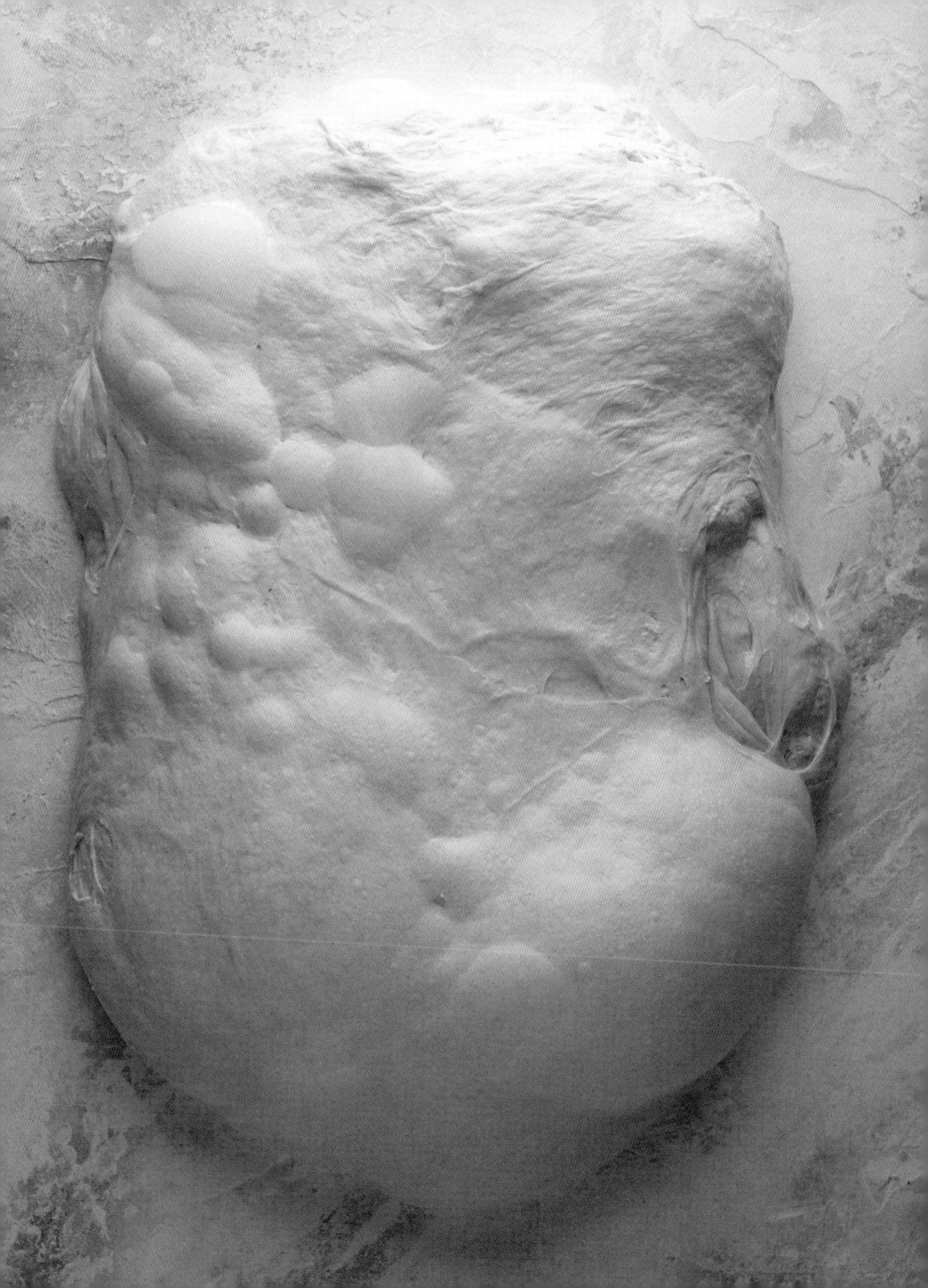

# Village Sourdough

*Lamarina* bread is a sourdough bread that is formed and baked in large metallic shallow trays. It's a traditional baking technique that is still found in old island bakeries. Baked in this way, the bread is fluffy and textured inside while the crust, where it touches the tray, is very crisp. Usually, it contains yellow and rye flours to impart a deep flavour, and it is shaped into a big flat loaf that fills the tray, then is left to rise, cut into portions and finally baked. This gives the loaf a great texture after baking. The raising agent for the dough is the starter, not the yeast, which makes it more natural. The starter is your best friend – just feed it every now and then to help it grow as it gets sour.

**SERVES 2**

**RYE STARTER:**
200g rye flour, sifted
200ml water, at room temperature

**LEVAIN STARTER:**
150g rye starter (see above)
150ml water, at room temperature
150g strong white bread flour (T55), sifted

**'TIGER' CRAQUELIN:**
90g rice flour, sifted
15g caster sugar
1 tsp fine salt
5g fast-action dried yeast
80ml water, at room temperature
35ml extra-virgin olive oil

**VILLAGE SOURDOUGH**
500g strong white bread flour, sifted
225g Caputo semola yellow flour, sifted, plus extra for dusting
100g dark rye flour, sifted
20g fine salt
15g caster sugar
500ml water, chilled
10g fresh yeast
levain starter (see above)
50ml extra-virgin olive oil, plus extra for brushing

**RYE STARTER**

Make the rye starter: in a bowl, stir the rye flour and the water until well combined. Transfer to a container, cover with a lid and set aside at room temperature for 1 day until it is bubbly and doubled in size. It is now ready to use for baking, or you can store it in the fridge.

**LEVAIN STARTER**

Make the levain starter: in a bowl, mix all the ingredients by hand until a coarse dough is formed. Transfer to a container, cover with a lid and set aside to rest at room temperature for 1 hour.

**NOTE**: You only use 150g of the 400g rye starter to make this loaf. Keep the leftover rye starter and feed it with 100ml water and 100g rye flour to make more starter for future use. Every time you use some of your rye starter, feed it again with equal parts of water and rye flour.

**'TIGER' CRAQUELIN**

Make the tiger craquelin: put the rice flour, sugar and salt in a bowl and mix together with a whisk. Dissolve the yeast in the water and add to the dry ingredients, whisking until well combined. Mix in the olive oil, cover with cling film and set aside in the fridge.

**VILLAGE SOURDOUGH**

Make the bread: in a food mixer bowl, whisk by hand the three flours, salt and sugar until well combined. Then attach the bowl to the mixer, fitted with the dough hook attachment.

Put the water and fresh yeast in a jug and whisk until the yeast dissolves.

With the mixer running on medium speed, gradually add the yeast mixture, a little at a time, until a dough starts to form. Add the levain starter in batches and continue mixing for 15 minutes, or until well combined. Gradually add the olive oil and mix for 2 minutes. Stop the mixer, scrape down the dough and continue mixing for 3 minutes, or until a firm dough is formed.

Transfer to a lightly oiled large bowl and cover with a clean tea towel. Set aside at room temperature for 2 hours, or until well risen.

Brush a rectangular baking tray, 30 x 40cm and 6cm deep, with olive oil and dust with semola flour, removing any excess flour. Transfer the risen dough to a clean work surface, dusted with flour, and quickly fold it over four times to remove the air. Place the dough in the oiled tray. Lightly oil your fingertips and press down on the dough to spread it out evenly on the tray.

Use your oven as a proofer by placing a shallow pan of water at the bottom and preheating it to 50°C, or the lowest temperature possible for gas (leaving the gas oven door slightly open). Place the pan in the oven and proof for 45 minutes, or until doubled in size.

Remove from the oven and increase the temperature to 180°C fan (200°C), gas mark 6. Leave the pan of water in the oven.

Dip a dough scraper in olive oil and cut the dough through all the way to the bottom of the tray to make 12–15 equal-sized pieces. Evenly spread the cold craquelin over the top of every piece.

Bake in the preheated oven for 45 minutes, remove the pan of water and continue baking for a further 30 minutes, or until golden brown.

Remove the bread from the oven and leave on the tray to cool down at room temperature. Use it within 2 days.

# Vasilopita (New Year Cake)

Vasilopita is a traditional Greek cake, which is baked the day before the New Year celebrations. It always contains a hidden coin or lucky charm symbolizing good fortune. It is customarily served after midnight on New Year's Eve, or the following day, and whoever finds the coin in their slice is believed to be blessed with good luck and prosperity in the coming year. It is named after the fourth-century bishop Saint Basil (Vassilis) who distributed gold coins in sweetened bread to the poor.

**SERVES 8**

120g eggs (2 large eggs)
160g caster sugar
100g full-fat Greek yoghurt
50ml sunflower oil, plus extra for brushing
35ml extra-virgin olive oil
85ml orange juice, strained
grated zest of 2 oranges
¼ tsp bicarbonate of soda
225g plain flour, sifted
3 tsp baking powder
½ tsp ground cloves
1 tsp ground cinnamon
100g walnuts, roughly chopped
200g sultanas, soaked overnight in white rum and strained
icing sugar, for dusting
edible gold leaf (optional)

In a food mixer, fitted with the whisk attachment, beat the eggs and sugar until frothy and creamy. Add the yoghurt and mix well.

In a bowl, mix together the sunflower and olive oils, orange juice, orange zest and bicarbonate of soda.

In another bowl, mix together the flour, baking powder and spices.

Preheat the oven to 180°C fan (200°C), gas mark 6. Lightly brush a 1kg round cake tin of 18cm diameter with sunflower oil and line it with baking paper.

Change the whisk to the paddle attachment on the food mixer and add the oil and orange juice mixture. Mix until well combined and then add the flour and spice mixture. Mix well to incorporate. Lastly, add the walnuts and sultanas and mix until they are distributed evenly throughout the cake mixture.

Transfer the mixture to the prepared cake tin and bake in the preheated oven for 40 minutes. To check if the cake is ready, insert the tip of a knife into the centre – if it comes out clean, the cake is cooked. If not, place it back in the oven for a few more minutes and check again.

Leave the cake in the tin to cool down at room temperature. When cold, remove from the tin and dust with sifted icing sugar. Top with edible gold leaf (if using).

**TIP**: Hide a coin by inserting it into the base of the cake after baking and before dusting with the icing sugar.

# Tahini Brioche

Brioche is such a lovely bread to bake. We have added a Greek touch with tahini and thyme honey to enhance the flavour. The following steps explain how to make buns for burgers where the sweetness of the bread pairs wonderfully with the savoury beef patties. You can also shape the dough into loaves for slicing for sandwiches or toast for breakfast and brunch.

**MAKES 12 BUNS**

450g strong white bread flour, sifted, plus extra for dusting
10g fast-action dried yeast
10g fine salt
50g caster sugar
70ml full-fat milk
220g eggs (4 medium eggs)
160g unsalted butter, cubed
30g tahini
1 tbsp thyme honey

**NOTE**: To make the dough, all the ingredients must be at room temperature.

**FOR THE BUNS:**
3 medium egg yolks
60ml full-fat milk
100g sesame seeds

**FOR THE LOAF:**
melted unsalted butter, for brushing
2 medium egg yolks
40ml full-fat milk

In a food mixer bowl, whisk the flour, yeast, salt and sugar by hand until well combined. Attach the bowl to the mixer, fitted with the dough hook attachment.

Add the milk and eggs and mix for 20 minutes on medium speed until you have a smooth dough. Check for the 'dough window effect' (see page 211) before moving on to the next step.

Gradually add the butter, a little at a time, while mixing for 5–10 minutes. When the butter is incorporated, scrape down the hook and the sides and bottom of the bowl. Add the tahini and honey and mix for 10–15 minutes, or until the dough is elastic and shiny, and sticks to the hook and bottom of the bowl.

Transfer the dough to a lightly floured bowl, cover with cling film and leave to rise at room temperature for 1 hour.

Remove the dough from the bowl and fold over twice. Return to the bowl, cover with cling film and leave in the fridge overnight.

The next day, remove the dough from the fridge, fold it over once and then divide into 12 equal-sized (80g) portions. Keep it cool while you're working and roll each portion quickly into a ball. Take care not to overwork the dough to prevent the butter melting. Place the buns on some baking trays lined with baking paper, spacing them 10cm apart.

Meanwhile, use your oven as a proofer by placing a shallow pan of water at the bottom and preheating it to 50°C, or the lowest temperature possible for gas (leaving the gas oven door slightly open). Place the buns in the oven for 45 minutes to proof them.

Remove the buns and increase the oven temperature to 180°C fan (200°C), gas mark 6. Leave the pan of water in the oven.

Mix the egg yolks and milk in a bowl and gently brush the mixture over the top of each proofed bun. Sprinkle with sesame seeds.

Bake the buns in the preheated oven for 8 minutes, or until golden brown. Remove from the oven and set aside to cool down at room temperature. Use the same day.

MAKES 1 X 1KG LOAF

**FOR THE LOAF**

Make the recipe above until step 5.

The following day, remove the dough from the fridge and fold it over once. Roll into a thick log to fit a rectangular 1kg brioche loaf tin. Brush the pan lightly with butter and place the dough inside. Leave to rest for 10 minutes at room temperature.

Use your oven as a proofer as described in step 7 above. Proof the loaf in the oven for 1 hour, then remove and increase the oven temperature to 180°C fan (200°C), gas mark 6. Leave the pan of water in the oven.

Mix the egg yolks and milk in a bowl and gently brush the mixture over the top of the loaf. Bake in the preheated oven for 40–50 minutes, or until golden brown on top. Remove the loaf from the pan and leave on a wire rack to cool at room temperature. Cut into slices to serve. Store the loaf at room temperature, wrapped in cling film, for up to 2 days.

# Cinnamon Rolls

One day in March 2022, we received an email from a young woman, a professional pastry chef, who lived in a country where war had just erupted, asking for our help to relocate to London. A few months later, we managed to get her a visa and she came to work at one of our restaurants. One day, the kitchen was filled with the breath-taking aroma of baked dough, caramelized sugar and cinnamon – she was making cinnamon rolls for the staff's breakfast. We knew immediately that we had to develop this recipe and share it with our guests. This was the birth of our brunch cinnamon rolls.

**SERVES 8**

400g strong white bread flour, sifted, plus extra for dusting
10g fine salt
60g caster sugar
15g fresh yeast
250g eggs (5 medium eggs)
200g unsalted butter, cubed
oil, for brushing
120g light brown sugar
20g ground cinnamon
melted unsalted butter, for brushing
icing sugar, for dusting

**NOTE**: To make the dough, all the ingredients must be at room temperature.

**HONEY SYRUP:**
150g caster sugar
170ml water
60g thyme honey

**ALMOND CREAM:**
90g unsalted butter, cubed
90g caster sugar
90g ground almonds
90g eggs (2 small eggs)
2 tsp vanilla extract
¼ tsp fine salt

Make the dough: in a food mixer fitted with the dough hook attachment, mix the flour, salt, sugar, yeast and eggs on medium speed for 15 minutes – they will come together to form a dough. Gradually add the butter, while mixing, until fully incorporated, and then mix for another 10 minutes. Knead the dough until the 'dough window effect' (see page 211) is obtained.

Transfer the dough to a lightly oiled bowl, cover with cling film and leave to rest at room temperature for 1 hour.

Remove the dough from the bowl and fold it over twice. Return to the bowl, then cover with cling film and leave to rest in the fridge overnight.

Make the honey syrup: put all the ingredients in a saucepan and bring to the boil, whisking well to dissolve the sugar. Remove the pan from the heat, cover with cling film and leave to cool at room temperature. When cool, strain into a container and keep in the fridge until required.

Make the almond cream: in a food mixer, using the whisk attachment, mix the butter, sugar and ground almonds until well combined. Add the eggs, one at a time, while mixing, and continue mixing for 3 minutes. Add the vanilla extract and salt and mix for 1 minute. Transfer to a container with a lid and keep in the fridge until required.

The following day, remove the dough from the fridge and divide into two equal-sized portions.

On a flour-dusted surface, roll out each portion of dough with a rolling pin into a 50 x 30cm rectangle that is 1cm thick. Trim the edges to ensure a perfect rectangular shape.

Spread the almond cream evenly on top of each rectangle and sprinkle with light brown sugar and cinnamon.

Starting from the long edge, tightly roll up each rectangle into a log shape. Cut each log into 4cm-thick slices – you should end up with 24 sliced rolls.

Brush eight cast iron pans or baking tins (8–10cm diameter) with melted butter and place three rolls in each pan with the rolled side facing up, so you can see the filling.

Use your oven as a proofer by placing a shallow pan of water at the bottom and preheating it to 50°C, or the lowest temperature possible for gas (leaving the gas oven door slightly open). Place the pans in the oven and proof for 1 hour.

Remove the pans and increase the oven temperature to 180°C fan (200°C), gas mark 6. Leave the tray of water in the oven.

Bake the rolls for 15 minutes, then remove the pan of water and continue baking for 8 minutes. Remove from the oven, then glaze the cinnamon rolls with honey syrup and leave to cool at room temperature. Once cool, carefully remove the cinnamon rolls from the pans, dust with icing sugar and serve.

**TIP: DOUGH WINDOW EFFECT**

The dough must be elastic, smooth, and stretchy.

To check if the dough is ready to shape and bake, take a small piece of dough, roll in between your palms and then gently stretch it between your fingers. If the dough is well developed, it should stretch into a thin, translucent membrane without tearing. This membrane should be strong enough to let light pass through it, resembling a windowpane.

If the dough tears easily or doesn't stretch well, it will need more mixing or kneading to help develop the gluten network. Achieving the dough window effect indicates that the gluten strands in the dough have developed properly, resulting in a better texture, rise, and structure when baked.

# Pitta Flatbreads

Inspired by our pitta bread heritage we have developed a recipe, which can be cooked in many different ways. It lends itself perfectly to oven cooking resulting in fluffy and airy pitta breads which are ideal for serving alongside spreads and dips. They can also be used as bases for mini pizzas. Adding some garlic and butter transforms them into the perfect garlic bread, while grilling over charcoal gives it a charred neutrality. Start with the basic recipe to understand the dough's behaviour, then unleash your creativity to craft some unique variations.

**MAKES 16 PITTA FLATBREADS**

2g fresh yeast
600ml water, chilled
500g type 00 pizza flour, sifted
250g strong white bread flour, sifted, plus extra for dusting
20ml extra-virgin olive oil, plus extra for brishing
20g fine salt
flour, for dusting
sea salt flakes, for seasoning

**STARTER:**
120ml water, chilled
250g strong white bread flour, sifted
1g fresh yeast

Make the starter: place all the ingredients in a bowl and mix together by hand until they come together to form a coarse-textured dough. Transfer to a container, cover with a lid and leave for at least 1 day at room temperature (or 3 days in the fridge) before using. Make the pitta breads: add the fresh yeast to 450ml water and whisk to dissolve. Cut the starter into large pieces and place in the bowl of a food mixer with the water-yeast mixture and the flours. Using the dough hook attachment, mix on medium speed for 10 minutes, or until everything combines into a soft dough around the hook.

Mix the remaining 150ml water with the olive oil and salt in a jug. With the motor running, add this to the food mixer, a little at a time. Continue mixing until the dough is thoroughly kneaded but still moist. This will take 15–20 minutes. Check for the 'dough window effect' (see page 211) before moving on to the next step. Scrape down the dough, lightly oil your hands and transfer the dough to a lightly oiled bowl. Cover with cling film and rest overnight in the fridge. Remove the dough from the fridge and fold it over twice, on a flour dusted surface. Cut into 16 portions of 100g and roll into balls. Lightly dust a shallow rectangular container with flour and place the balls inside, leaving space between them to allow them to expand. Cover with a tea towel and set aside at room temperature for 20 minutes. Preheat the oven to 180°C fan (200°C), gas mark 6.

Line two baking trays with baking paper. On a surface, dusted with flour, stretch out each dough ball, pushing with your fingers to form a round pitta. Brush with olive oil, sprinkle with sea salt. Transfer to the lined baking trays and bake in the preheated oven for 6–8 minutes, or until the pitta breads are light brown and puffed up – they should be soft rather than crisp. Remove from the oven and let them cool a little on the baking trays. Enjoy them warm.

# Tsoureki

Tsoureki is the Greek brioche, a hearty sweet bread that is made with butter and the magic kick of mastiha and mahlepi, a spice made from the seeds of mahaleb cherries. Most commonly, it is shaped into braided loaves and it can be enjoyed in many different ways: as a sweetened toastie with cheese and ham, or topped with chocolate spread or butter and jelly, or, best of all, dipped in milk.

**MAKES 8 TSOUREKI**

100ml water, chilled
20g fresh yeast
650g strong white bread flour, sifted, plus extra for dusting
100ml full-fat milk
10 drops of mastic essence
3 tsp mahlepi powder (mahaleb)
60ml orange juice, strained
grated zest of 1 orange
180g eggs (3 large eggs)
160g caster sugar
70g unsalted butter, cubed, at room temperature

**TO SERVE:**
120g clotted cream
80g sour cherries in syrup
120g milk chocolate cream (*see page 277*)

Pour the chilled water into a bowl, add the yeast and stir until dissolved. Add 150g flour and mix by hand until you have a coarse-textured dough. Transfer this 'starter' to a bowl, dusted with flour, then cover with a clean tea towel and set aside for 1 hour at room temperature.

Put the milk, mastic essence, mahlepi, orange juice and zest in a bowl and whisk well.

Using the whisk attachment on a food mixer, beat the eggs and sugar until frothy, creamy and tripled in volume. Add the milk mixture and continue whisking until well combined.

Replace the whisk with the hook attachment and, with the motor running on low speed, gradually add the remaining 500g flour, a little at a time, for 3–5 minutes, or until a dough starts to form. Immediately add the starter mixture, in batches, and after adding the last batch, mix for 10–15 minutes, or until the dough is firm and sticking to the hook.

Gradually add the butter and continue mixing for 10–15 minutes. You will end up with an elastic and sticky dough that sticks onto the hook.

Scrape down the dough and transfer to a lightly floured bowl. Cover with a tea towel and leave to rest at room temperature for 2 hours, or until it triples in size.

Transfer the dough to a clean flour-dusted surface, and fold over 3–4 times to remove the air. The dough will be sticky, so make sure you have plenty of flour on the work surface and your hands. Separate the dough with a dough scraper into 24 portions (50g each) and gently roll them into balls. Use eight cast iron pans of 8–10cm diameter and 8cm deep and place three balls in each pan.

Use your oven as a proofer by placing a shallow pan of water in the bottom and preheat to 50°C, or the lowest temperature possible for gas (leaving the gas oven door slightly open). Place the cast iron pans in the oven and proof for 1 hour.

**EGG WASH:**
1 large egg, beaten
20ml water

Remove the cast iron pans with the proofed tsourekia from the oven and increase the temperature to 180°C fan (200°C), gas mark 6.

Make the egg wash: mix the egg and water together in a bowl and brush it lightly over the top of the proofed tsoureki dough. Bake in the preheated oven for 10 minutes, then remove the pan of water and bake for a further 8–10 minutes, or until golden brown.

Remove from the oven and leave to cool down at room temperature. When cool, remove the tsoureki from the pans by running a knife around the edges.

Serve with clotted cream and sour cherries in syrup or milk chocolate cream on the side.

## Desserts

224 Greek Coffe Tiramisu Profiteroles
228 Strawberry Pavlova
232 Moustokoulouro Sandwich & Alaska
236 Extra-Virgin Olive Oil Parfait
238 Baked Feta Cheesecake
240 Chocolate Tarts
244 Galaktoboureko

## Sweet Treats

250 Olive Oil Macarons
254 Chocolate Mosaic
256 Melomakarona Biscuits
258 Chocolate Halvas

# Pastry

# SWEET THINGS

For the ancient Greeks, pastry-making was elevated to an art form. Over the centuries, Greek pastry evolved through conquests, migrations and trade routes and was influenced by many cultures and culinary traditions. The influence of Ottoman cuisine introduced ingredients like filo (phyllo) dough, rose water, semolina and spices, giving rise to iconic desserts, such as baklava, galaktoboureko and ravani, with rich fillings of nuts, custard or cheese. With their delicate layers and sweet syrups, these desserts continue to captivate palates worldwide. Similarly, the Venetians and French brought techniques like custard-making and pastry layering, further enriching the Greek world of desserts.

In addition to their cultural significance, Greek desserts offer a glimpse into the country's rich agricultural heritage with foods sourced from land and sea. Extra-virgin olive oil, nuts, fruits, hand-picked sea salt and dairy products feature prominently in many recipes, highlighting the diversity of local ingredients, such as honey from the mountains of Crete, pistachios from Aegina Island, citrus fruits and figs from the sun-drenched groves of the Peloponnese, and mastiha (mastic), the unique spice that comes from the resin of the mastic trees that grow in only the southern part of Chios Island.

Beyond their culinary appeal, Greek sweets play a significant role in social and cultural traditions. Special occasions, such as weddings, baptisms, name days and feasts, are incomplete without a lavish spread of desserts. They are a hallmark of the Christmas festivities when families gather to share platters of seasonal sweets, including melomakarona (olive-oil based spiced biscuits soaked in honey syrup). They embody warmth, generosity and the Greek concept of xenia, rooted in the word philoxenia, which means hospitality.

*'As a cook I see no distinction between sweet and savoury. Both hold equal places in my mind and my heart, cherished with the same eagerness and commitment. During my degree in the culinary arts, pastry and baking were considered secondary to the savoury courses of the curriculum, but that has not been the case throughout my career and evolution as a chef. For me, crafting desserts and savoury dishes are intertwined and I cannot think of them differently. On my culinary journey, I approach both with the same love and enthusiasm, embracing the diversity of flavours and techniques with equal excitement. For me, there is no line between them, only the joy of creating delicious gastronomic experiences that captivate the senses and evoke emotions to our guests.'*

**NIKOS**

# DESSERTS

Greek desserts are a tapestry of flavours and history based on recipes passed down through generations and telling the story of a nation through its sweet creations. In this chapter you will enjoy making modern Greek desserts that introduce a contemporary twist on some traditional favourites, infusing classic recipes with innovation and creativity, blending international signature dishes with a modern Greek spirit to create recipes that play with flavours and have been cherished throughout the years.

*'I have always been captivated by classic recipes and the ways they can be reimagined while preserving their essence. Fuelled by my passion for coffee and my love for the timeless dessert, Tiramisu, we created an innovative twist on the traditional recipe. The dessert is called Greek Coffee Tiramisu Profiteroles and features a light mascarpone cream infused with Greek coffee, paired with a unique recipe for homemade pâte à choux that achieves a crispy yet fluffy texture. Topped with a delicate crumble of white chocolate and espresso, it offers a delightful fusion of flavours and textures.'*

**ANDREAS**

# Greek Coffee Tiramisu Profiteroles

Discover a dessert that marries two iconic sweets from around the globe with the rich flavour of Greek coffee. This recipe shows you how to make perfect choux pastry as well as luscious coffee cream. You'll work with agar agar to learn how to craft smooth, glossy gels, and experience the bold and robust flavour of Greek coffee.

SERVES 5

**MASCARPONE COFFEE CREAM:**
- 4g gelatine sheets
- 10g espresso coffee beans, crushed
- 1 shot strained Greek coffee (or espresso coffee)
- 200ml single cream
- 60g egg yolks (3 medium egg yolks)
- 40g caster sugar
- 300g mascarpone cheese

**MILK CHOCOLATE CREAM:**
- 6g gelatine sheets
- 200g milk chocolate (40% cocoa solids), cut into small pieces
- 100ml full-fat milk
- 1 tsp glucose syrup
- 200ml double cream (cold)

**AMARETTO PUDDING:**
- 150ml simple syrup (*see page 276*)
- 50ml water
- ½ tsp agar agar
- ½ tsp Cointreau
- 1 tsp lime juice, strained
- 100ml Amaretto liqueur

**COCOA CRAQUELIN:**
- 70g soft light brown sugar
- 10g cocoa powder
- 60g plain flour, sifted
- 60g unsalted butter, cubed, at room temperature

Make the mascarpone coffee cream: soak the gelatine sheets in a bowl of iced cold water until softened. Put the coffee beans, shot of coffee and the cream in a saucepan and set over a low heat. When it starts to simmer, remove from the heat, cover the top of the pan with cling film and leave to steep for 10 minutes.

Meanwhile, put the egg yolks and sugar in a bowl and whisk by hand until creamy. Strain the warm coffee cream into the egg yolk mixture and whisk to incorporate. Return to the pan and set over a medium heat. With a rubber spatula, stir continuously, scraping the bottom of the pan, until the temperature of the mixture is 82°C on a sugar thermometer. Immediately, take the pan off the heat (this prevents the eggs from scrambling) and strain through a fine sieve into a container. Gently squeeze any water out of the softened gelatine and add to the mixture. Whisk until the gelatine dissolves.

Set aside and when the temperature drops to 40°C, add the mascarpone, whisking by hand until well combined. Strain into a bowl, then cover with cling film, attached to the surface, and leave in the fridge for 12 hours, or until set. Once set, whisk gently to refresh the cream and transfer to a piping bag. Reserve in the fridge.

Make the milk chocolate cream: soak the gelatine sheets in a bowl of iced water until softened. Meanwhile, melt the chocolate in the microwave or in a bowl suspended over a pan of simmering water (without the bowl touching the water).

Warm the milk and glucose in a saucepan set over a low to medium heat. Mix to dissolve the glucose and remove from the heat. Squeeze out the water from the softened gelatine and add to the pan, whisking until dissolved. Strain through a sieve over the melted chocolate and mix gently with a rubber spatula.

Transfer the mixture to a plastic jug and start mixing with a hand-held electric blender, adding the double cream, until well combined and

**COFFEE CRUMBLE:**

80g plain flour, sifted
25g cornflour
30g caster sugar
½ tsp sea salt flakes
55g unsalted butter, melted
100g white chocolate, melted
120g milk powder
10g ground espresso coffee

**CHOUX PASTRY (MAKES 35 PROFITEROLES):**

35ml full-fat milk
35ml water
30g unsalted butter, cubed, cold
a pinch of fine salt
1 tsp caster sugar
50g plain flour, sifted
2 small free-range eggs

**TO GARNISH:**

cocoa powder, for dusting

shiny. The jug will help to keep the blender fully submerged in the mixture and prevent air bubbles.

Transfer to a bowl, cover with cling film, attached to the surface, and leave in the fridge for at least 12 hours until set. Once set, whisk gently to refresh the cream and transfer to a piping bag fitted with a round nozzle. Keep in the fridge until required.

Make the amaretto pudding: put the simple syrup, water and agar agar in a saucepan set over a medium heat and bring to the boil. Cook, whisking continuously, for 1–2 minutes to activate the agar agar. Remove the pan from the heat and whisk in the remaining ingredients. Strain into a container, cover with cling film and leave in the fridge for 2 hours until set and jellified.

Transfer the jelly to a blender and blend on medium speed until creamy and shiny. Place in a squeezy bottle and keep in the fridge for up to 5 days.

Make the cocoa craquelin: put the sugar, cocoa and flour in a bowl and whisk by hand. Gradually add the butter a little at a time, mixing constantly, until a soft dough forms. On a clean surface, knead by hand into a smooth ball.

Place the dough between two sheets of baking paper and roll it out until 3mm thick. Place in the fridge for 20 minutes to cool. Remove the top sheet of paper and, using a 3cm biscuit cutter, cut out 35 circles of dough. Cover again with the baking paper and place in the freezer until required.

Preheat the oven to 180°C fan (200°C), gas mark 4. Line a baking tray with baking paper.

Make the coffee crumble: using the paddle attachment on a food mixer, mix the flour, cornflour, sugar and sea salt. Add the melted butter and mix until thick and crumbly.

Spread the crumble out evenly on the lined baking tray and bake in the preheated oven for 15 minutes, or until golden brown. Remove and set aside to cool at room temperature. Do not turn the oven off.

Transfer the crumble to a bowl and mix in the melted white chocolate with a spatula. Gradually fold in the milk powder and the ground coffee. Freeze for 10 minutes and then store in a sealed container in the fridge until required.

Make the choux pastry: put the milk, water, butter, salt and sugar in a saucepan set over a medium heat. Bring to the boil, stirring with a rubber spatula. Remove from the heat and start adding the flour, a little at a time, using the spatula until the mixture forms a light dough that does not stick to the sides of the pan. Set the pan over a low to medium heat and cook for 4–5 minutes, stirring, or until the dough is cooked and shiny. Remove from the heat and transfer the dough to a food mixer fitted with the paddle attachment.

Start mixing and add an egg. When it is fully incorporated, add the remaining egg and mix for about 10 minutes, or until the dough is glossy and smooth.

Transfer to a piping bag fitted with a round 10mm nozzle and pipe 35 small balls of dough (the size of a cherry) onto a baking tray lined with baking paper, leaving plenty of space in between them. Top each ball with a frozen disc of cocoa craquelin. Bake in the preheated oven for 15–20 minutes, or until well risen, puffed up and golden. To test whether the profiteroles are cooked, tap one with your knuckles – it should sound hollow. Leave to cool at room temperature and transfer to a container. Keep at room temperature and use the same day.

When you are ready to serve the profiteroles, make a hole in the underside of each choux ball and fill with the milk chocolate cream.

Pipe eight dollops of mascarpone coffee cream onto a serving dish in a daisy shape, making the central dollop larger than the other seven around it. Squeeze out a large dot of amaretto pudding between the coffee cream dollops. Place seven filled profiteroles around the central dollop and on top of the seven dollops. Sprinkle the coffee crumble in the middle. Dust with cocoa powder and serve. Repeat for the remaining four dishes.

# Strawberry Pavlova

As a nation, we Greeks eagerly anticipate the arrival of seasonal fruits, so we can incorporate them into our daily diet. Spring heralds the arrival of juicy strawberries, with Greece being a significant producer, especially in the Peloponnese. Further north in forested mountainous areas you can find wild varieties with a distinctive aroma and deep flavour. Despite the availability of many fruits all-the-year-round, we still cherish the connection to seasonal produce and varieties, which help us to discern the changing seasons.

**SERVES 6**

250g caster sugar
80ml water
a pinch of sea salt flakes
90g egg whites (3 medium egg whites)
24 strawberries, quartered
42 small mint leaves
1½ limes

**VANILLA CREAM:**
5g gelatine sheets
150g white chocolate
65ml full-fat milk
1 tsp vanilla extract with seeds
20g egg yolk (1 medium egg yolk)
1 tsp caster sugar
250ml double cream

**CITRUS CURD:**
110g caster sugar
60ml lemon juice, strained
20ml lime juice, strained
grated zest of ½ lemon
grated zest of ½ lime
100g eggs (2 medium eggs)
125g unsalted butter, cubed, at room temperature

**STRAWBERRY SAUCE:**
250g strawberries, stemmed
100g caster sugar
2 tsp glucose syrup
2 thin slices of lemon peel
10 mint leaves, chopped
1 tsp lime juice, strained
grated zest of 1 lime

Make the vanilla cream: leave the gelatine sheets to soak in a bowl of iced cold water until softened.

Meanwhile, melt the chocolate in the microwave or in a bain-marie

Make a crème anglaise by warming the milk and vanilla extract in a saucepan set over a medium heat. In another bowl, whisk the egg yolk and sugar until creamy. Pour the warm milk into the egg mixture and whisk to incorporate. Return to the pan and cook gently over a low heat, stirring constantly with a rubber spatula, until the mixture thickens and reaches 80°C.

Immediately, remove from the heat, squeeze the water out of the softened gelatine and stir into the crème anglaise. Strain through a fine sieve into the bowl containing the melted chocolate and mix well.

Transfer to a plastic jug and start mixing with a hand-held electric blender, gradually adding the double cream, until well incorporated and shiny. Using a jug will help to keep the blender fully submerged and prevent air bubbles forming. Transfer to a bowl, then cover with cling film, attached to the surface. Chill in the fridge for 12 hours until set. Once set, whisk gently to refresh the vanilla cream and transfer to a piping bag. Keep in the fridge until required.

Make the citrus curd: place the sugar, lemon and lime juice and zest and eggs in a saucepan set over a medium heat. Whisk constantly until the mixture thickens.

Remove from the heat, strain through a fine sieve into a plastic jug and start mixing with a hand-held electric blender, gradually adding the butter, until incorporated and shiny. Try to keep the blender submerged in the mixture to prevent air bubbles. Transfer to a container and cover with cling film, attached to the surface. Chill in the fridge for at least

12 hours, or until the curd sets. Once set, transfer to a piping bag and keep in the fridge for up to 3 days.

Make the strawberry sauce: blitz the strawberries in a blender to a smooth purée. Transfer to a saucepan and stir in the sugar, glucose syrup and lemon peel. Set over a high heat and bring to the boil, then reduce the heat to low and cook for 5 minutes, or until the mixture thickens. Remove from the heat, transfer to a jug and add the mint, lime juice and zest. Blend with a hand-held electric blender until smooth. Strain into a container or squeezy bottle and keep in the fridge for up to 5 days.

Make the meringue: put the sugar, water and sea salt flakes in a saucepan set over a medium heat. Bring to the boil, swirling the pan occasionally, and boil until the syrup starts to caramelize at 118°C (check with a sugar thermometer).

Meanwhile (before the sugar caramelizes), beat the egg whites in a food mixer until soft peaks form. As soon as the caramel reaches 118°C, remove the pan from the heat and start pouring it in a thin stream over the egg whites, whisking all the time until the mixture is glossy and the temperature has decreased to 45°C.

Preheat the oven to 80°C fan. Line a baking tray with baking paper.

Using two soup spoons, make six meringue nests, hollowing out the centre a little and creating some peaks on the top outer edge. Place the nests on the lined baking tray, about 10cm apart.

Bake in the preheated oven for 1 hour 30 minutes–2 hours, or until the meringues are crisp outside and fluffy inside. Remove from the oven and set aside to cool down at room temperature.

Just before serving, pipe some citrus curd and some vanilla cream in the centre of each meringue nest. Arrange four quartered strawberries on top and drizzle with the strawberry sauce. Decorate with seven small mint leaves and freshly grate some lime zest over the top. Place each pavlova on a serving plate and serve immediately.

# Moustokoulouro Sandwich & Alaska

*Moustokouloura* are traditional Greek cookies. The dough is made with grape must, which is the juice from freshly crushed grapes, together with the skins and seeds, in the initial process of winemaking. Throughout the centuries the surplus of grape must has inspired a myriad of delightful creations, from velvety *moustalevria*, a creamy delicacy, to the beloved moustokouloura cookies. Here our soft cookie-style moustokouloura can be made for an ice cream sandwich or topped with Italian meringue to reimagine the traditional Alaska dessert.

**SERVES 15**

900g salted caramel, pistachio or vanilla ice cream
250ml brewed espresso coffee, at room temperature
500g caster sugar
160ml water
180g egg whites (6 large egg whites)

**MOUSTOKOULOURO COOKIES (MAKES 15 COOKIES):**

200g plain flour, sifted
30g soft light brown sugar
1 tsp baking powder
½ tsp bicarbonate of soda
½ tsp ground cinnamon
¼ tsp ground cloves
a pinch of sea salt flakes
200g milk chocolate (40% cocoa solids), coarsely chopped
40g walnuts, roasted at 180°C fan (200°C), gas mark 6 for 6 minutes, roughly chopped
grated zest of ½ orange
70g molasses
70ml sunflower oil
70ml orange juice, strained
2 tsp thyme honey

**MOUSTOKOULOURO SANDWICH**

2 Moustokoulouro cookies
1 scoop of salted caramel ice cream
1 tbsp salted caramel sauce (see page 277)
1 walnut

Make the moustokoulouro cookies: using the paddle attachment on a food mixer, mix the flour, sugar, baking powder, bicarbonate of soda, ground spices, salt, chocolate, walnuts and orange zest.

Put the molasses, sunflower oil, orange juice and honey in a bowl and whisk by hand until well combined. Pour into the mixer, a little at a time, and mix until everything comes together and forms a soft dough – do not overwork the mixture.

Transfer to a container and cover with cling film, attached to the surface of the dough. Chill in the fridge for 30 minutes.

Preheat the oven to 180°C fan (200°C), gas mark 6. Line a baking tray with baking paper.

Divide the dough into 15 equal-sized portions and shape into balls. Place a 7cm cookie cutter on the lined baking tray and put a dough ball inside it. With your fingers, gently press by hand to spread the dough out inside the cutter and shape it into a cookie. Remove the cutter and repeat with the remaining dough balls, spacing them about 5cm apart.

Bake in the preheated oven for 6–10 minutes, or until the cookies are baked but still soft inside. Remove from the oven and leave on the baking tray to cool at room temperature.

**MOUSTOKOULOURO SANDWICH**

Make a speedy dessert, by placing a scoop of salted caramel ice cream between two moustokoulouro cookies.

Drizzle with 1 tablespoon salted caramel sauce and top with the walnut.

**MOUSTOKOULOURO ALASKA**

Trim the edges of the cookies with the 7cm cookie cutter.

Fill 15 x 7cm-diameter semi-sphere moulds (three-quarters full) with ice cream, levelling the top with a spatula. Take a cookie and dip into the espresso coffee, then gently press onto the ice cream. Repeat with the remaining cookies. Chill in the freezer for at least 1 hour.

Make the Italian meringue: put the sugar and water in a saucepan and set over a medium heat. Bring to the boil, swirling the pan occasionally, and boil until the syrup caramelizes at 118°C (check with a sugar thermometer).

Meanwhile (before the sugar caramelizes), whisk the egg whites in a food mixer until soft peaks form. As soon as the caramel reaches 118°C, remove the pan from the heat and start pouring it in a thin stream over the egg whites, whisking all the time until the mixture is glossy and the temperature has decreased to 45°C. Transfer to a piping bag fitted with a small nozzle.

Unmould a moustokouloro Alaska and pipe some meringue on top. Using a teaspoon, make some attractive peaks and spikes.

Quickly torch the meringue with a blowtorch, then repeat with the remaining Alaskas. Serve immediately while the ice cream is cold.

# Extra-Virgin Olive Oil Parfait

Inspired by Thessaloniki's dessert *Armenovil*, which is derived from Armenia's culinary heritage, we have created a dish that combines our beloved parfait and semifreddo textures in one recipe. It's served with a refreshing cherry syrup and finished with a drizzle of extra-virgin olive oil. The complementary flavours are elevated to new sensory heights by the addition of olive oil, which can be a valuable ingredient in sweet as well as savoury dishes.

### SERVES 4

50g caster sugar
40g blanched almonds, roasted at 180°C fan (200°C), gas mark 6 for 6 minutes
20g pistachios, roasted at 180°C fan (200°C), gas mark 6 for 6 minutes
200ml double cream
50ml single cream
1 tsp vanilla extract with seeds
125ml condensed milk
40g bitter chocolate (66% cocoa solids), coarsely grated
4 Maraschino cherries, each cut into 4 pieces
2 tbsp extra-virgin olive oil
12 drops of bitter almond essence
edible gold leaf (optional)

### CHERRY SOUP:

140g cherries, stemmed and pitted
200ml water
65g sour cherries in syrup
5g whole black peppercorns

Make the cherry soup: blitz the cherries and water to a smooth purée. Transfer to a saucepan and add the remaining ingredients. Cook over a low heat for 20–25 minutes, or until the mixture thickens. Strain into a squeezy bottle and keep in the fridge until required.

Put the sugar in a saucepan set over a medium heat and cook, swirling the pan occasionally, until it becomes a golden caramel. Add the roasted nuts and mix with a rubber spatula until combined. Spread evenly on a tray lined with baking paper and leave to cool at room temperature. Once cool, transfer to a zipper bag and smash with a rolling pin until you have a caramel crumble.

Whisk the double and single cream in a food mixer, using the whisk attachment, until it forms soft peaks. Whisk in the vanilla extract and condensed milk, stopping just before the stiff peak stage. Using a rubber spatula, gently fold in the caramel crumble and grated chocolate, taking care not to overwork the mixture.

Divide the parfait mixture between four semi-sphere moulds and chill in the freezer until frozen.

Turn out each parfait portion into a bowl straight from the freezer and garnish each with 1 Maraschino cherry. Pour 2 tablespoons of the cold sour cherry syrup around each parfait and drizzle with ½ tablespoon of olive oil and 3 drops of bitter almond essence. Garnish the parfait with gold leaf (if using) and serve immediately.

DESSERTS  Pastry 237

# Baked Feta Cheesecake

Baked cheesecake is a classic, and many people's favourite dessert, no matter where they are from and their culinary backgrounds. We have tried so many throughout the years but, even so, we were still searching for a unique recipe with a Greek touch and a deliciously moist and creamy texture. We finally landed on the perfect cheesecake by using barrel-matured feta cheese and pairing it with sour cherries in syrup. This unique recipe is so easy to prepare and cook; you only have to make it once and you'll be addicted to its simplicity as well as the final stunning result.

**SERVES 8**

- 125g barrel-matured soft feta cheese
- 415g Philadelphia cream cheese
- 130g icing sugar, sifted
- 25g cornflour, sifted
- 150ml single cream
- 130ml double cream
- 150g eggs (3 medium free-range eggs)
- 2 tsp vanilla extract with seeds
- 1 tsp sea salt flakes
- 160g sour cherries in syrup (or any fruit preserve of your choice)

Preheat the oven to 210°C fan (230°C), gas mark 8. Wrap the base and sides of an 18cm-diameter loose-bottomed cake tin with baking paper and then kitchen foil. Fold the excess foil tightly around the sides to ensure that both the baking paper and foil are snug and secure. Place on a baking tray.

Using the paddle attachment on a food mixer, mix the soft feta until creamy. Add the cream cheese and icing sugar and continue mixing until combined. Be careful not to overmix or it will curdle.

Put the cornflour and single cream in a bowl and hand whisk until smooth. Transfer to the mixer together with the double cream, eggs, vanilla extract and sea salt. Mix for 2–3 minutes, or until the mixture is silky and shiny – do not overwork the mixture.

Pour the mixture into the lined cake tin and bake in the preheated oven for 20–25 minutes, or until well risen, browned and the edges have cracked. Remove from the oven and leave for 1 hour at room temperature to cool down. Transfer to the fridge and chill for 3 hours, or until set.

Unwrap the foil and baking paper and carefully remove the cheesecake from the tin. Serve cut into slices with a spoonful of sour cherries in syrup. The cheesecake will keep well in the fridge for up to 2 days wrapped in cling film.

**TIP**: The trick is to bake the cheesecake on a high temperature, so it gets nicely coloured on top but is smooth and creamy inside.

# Chocolate Tarts

Tarts were a thing in Greece back in the 1990s. All pastry shops had dozens of tarts on display, in different sizes filled with various creams, coated with rustic jellies and topped with all kinds of fruits. It was a time when crème pâtissière reigned. Even today a special tart is always on display in the best pastry shops of the country. Proud of this tart dough, we present to you two different tart fillings based on white and milk chocolate.

**SERVES 5**

**TART SHELLS:**
- 100g icing sugar, sifted
- 120g unsalted butter, cubed, cold
- ½ tsp vanilla extract with seeds
- 35g egg (1 small free-range egg)
- a pinch of fine salt
- 35g almond powder (finely ground almonds)
- 250g plain flour, sifted
- melted unsalted butter, for brushing

Make the tart shells: using the paddle attachment on a food mixer, mix the icing sugar and cold butter on medium speed until creamy. Mix in the vanilla extract, while continuing to mix, and then add the egg and mix until incorporated. (If you are making a larger quantity, add the eggs one by one). Mix in the salt and almond powder and then gradually add the flour, mixing until a dough forms.

Shape the dough into a ball and wrap in cling film. Leave to rest in the fridge for 2 hours.

Preheat the oven to 180°C fan (200°C), gas mark 6. Line a baking tray with baking paper.

Place a sheet of baking paper on a clean work surface and put the chilled dough on top. Cover with another sheet of baking paper and roll out until it is 3mm thick. Transfer to the freezer and chill for 30 minutes.

Brush five 11cm tart rings with melted butter and place them on the lined baking tray.

Take the rolled dough out of the freezer and remove the baking paper on top. Using a tart ring, cut out five circles of dough for the bases of the tarts. Place a circle of dough inside each prepared tart ring. Using a knife, cut out five long strips of dough. The width of the strips should be the same as the height of the tart rings. Line the inner sides of the tart rings with the strips, using your fingers to gently press the bottom edge of the pastry into the circle of dough on the bottom, to seal the tarts. Prick the base of each tart with a fork and chill in the fridge for 15 minutes.

Bake in the preheated oven for 15–20 minutes, or until the pastry is light brown and crisp. Remove from the oven and, using a small knife, separate the crust from the sides of the tart rings. Carefully remove the rings and leave the tarts to cool at room temperature. Set aside while you prepare your desired filling.

**MILK CHOCOLATE PEANUT TARTS:**

250g smooth peanut butter

150ml salted caramel sauce (see page 277)

25g roasted salted peanuts

5 tsp dark chocolate pearls (optional: coat pearls with copper-coloured pastry powder)

sea salt flakes, for sprinkling

**MILK CHOCOLATE TONKA CREAM:**

6g gelatine sheets

200g milk chocolate (40% cocoa solids), cut into small pieces

100ml full-fat milk

1 tsp glucose syrup

½ small tonka bean, grated with a Microplane

200ml double cream, cold

Make the milk chocolate tonka cream: soak the gelatine sheets in a bowl of iced water until softened.

Meanwhile, melt the chocolate in the microwave or in a bowl suspended over a pan of simmering water (the bowl should not touch the water).

Put the milk, glucose and grated tonka bean in a saucepan set over a low to medium heat and warm gently. Stir to combine and then remove from the heat. Squeeze out the water from the softened gelatine and add to the pan, whisking until dissolved. Strain through a fine sieve over the melted chocolate and mix gently with a rubber spatula.

Transfer the mixture to a plastic jug and mix with a hand-held electric blender, adding the double cream, until well incorporated and shiny – using a jug will help to keep the blender fully submerged and prevent air bubbles.

Transfer to a bowl, cover with cling film, attached to the surface, and leave in the fridge for at least 12 hours until set. Once set, whisk gently to refresh the cream, then transfer to a piping bag fitted with a star nozzle and keep in the fridge until required.

To serve, spread the peanut butter over the bottom of each tart. Cover with salted caramel sauce, and then pipe the milk chocolate tonka cream on top. Decorate with peanuts and chocolate pearls and sprinkle with a pinch of sea salt flakes.

**WHITE CHOCOLATE QUINCE TARTS:**

150ml salted caramel sauce (*see page 277*)
125g hazelnut crumble (*see page 276*)
grated zest of 1 orange
30 mint leaves

**WHITE CHOCOLATE & CHEESE CREAM:**

6g gelatine sheets
160g white chocolate, roughly chopped
100ml full-fat milk
½ tbsp glucose syrup
200g Philadelphia cream cheese

**POACHED QUINCES:**

200g caster sugar
25ml grenadine syrup
500ml water
1 clove
1 cinnamon stick
40g thyme honey
½ tsp vanilla extract with seeds
3 quinces, peeled, deseeded and quartered

Make the white chocolate and cheese cream: soak the gelatine sheets in a bowl of iced water until softened.

Meanwhile, melt the chocolate in the microwave or in a bowl suspended over a pan of simmering water (the bowl should not touch the water).

Place the milk and glucose in a saucepan set over a medium heat and warm gently, stirring until well combined. Remove from the heat. Squeeze the water out of the softened gelatine and add to the pan, whisking until dissolved. Strain over the melted chocolate and mix gently with a rubber spatula.

Transfer to a plastic jug and mix with a hand-held electric blender, gradually adding the cream cheese, until well incorporated and shiny – the jug will help to keep the blender fully submerged and prevent air bubbles.

Transfer into a bowl and cover with cling film, attached to the surface, and leave in the fridge for at least 12 hours until set. Once set, whisk gently to refresh the cream, transfer to a piping bag and keep in the fridge until required.

Preheat the oven to 180°C fan (200°C), gas mark 6.

Make the poached quinces: put all the ingredients except the quinces in a saucepan and set over a medium heat. Bring to the boil, whisking occasionally, until syrupy. Remove from the heat and pour into a small shallow baking tray. Add the quince quarters, cut-side down, ensuring that they are fully submerged in the syrup.

Cover with kitchen foil and bake in the preheated oven for 45–60 minutes, or until the quince is tender but not mushy. Transfer to a container with the syrup, wrap loosely with cling film and cool in the fridge.

To serve, spread the salted caramel sauce over the bottom of each tart. Cover with the white chocolate and cheese cream and flatten the surface. Sprinkle with hazelnut crumble. Cut the poached quince quarters into smaller pieces and arrange on top of the crumble, in the middle of each tart. Garnish with orange zest and mint leaves.

# Galaktoboureko

Inspired by Middle Eastern desserts, Greek syrupy desserts constitute a rich and flavourful part of Greek gastronomy. These desserts typically feature layers of crispy pastry, such as filo or kataifi, which become delightfully crisp in the oven before absorbing sweet syrup infused with honey, citrus and spices, imparting their distinct taste and texture. Favourites among these desserts include baklava, ravani, walnut pie, saragli and, of course, galaktoboureko – a sweet treat comprised of a semolina custard nestled between layers of crispy filo, all moistened by sweet syrup. In our take on galaktoboureko, a light custard is drenched in syrup and berries to give some freshness and acidity. A more delicate interpretation of one of our favourite classic Greek desserts.

**SERVES 4-6**

**GINGER SYRUP:**
50g caster sugar
25ml water
½ tsp glucose syrup
1 cinnamon stick
3g fresh root ginger (skin on), thinly sliced
1 long, thin slice of lemon peel

**RASPBERRY PUDDING:**
400g raspberries
100ml water
60g caster sugar
2 tsp vanilla extract with seeds
½ tbsp agar agar
a small handful of mint leaves, chopped
1 tsp lime juice, strained
grated zest of 2 limes

**SPICED FILO PASTRY:**
35g unsalted butter, melted
30g icing sugar
4 frozen filo pastry sheets, defrosted
½ tsp ground cinnamon
¼ tsp ground cloves

Make the ginger syrup: put all the ingredients except the lemon peel in a saucepan and set over a high heat. Bring to the boil, then reduce the heat to a simmer and stir until the sugar dissolves. Remove from the heat, add the lemon peel, cover with cling film and set aside at room temperature until cold. Strain into a container, then cover and chill in the fridge until required.

Make the raspberry pudding: blitz the raspberries in a blender until you have a smooth purée.

Transfer to a saucepan and add the water, sugar and vanilla extract. Set over a medium heat and whisk until the sugar dissolves. Stir in the agar agar, mint and lime juice and zest and bring to the boil. Reduce the heat to medium and cook for 2 minutes, or until the agar agar is activated and the mixture thickens.

Strain through a sieve into a container. Cover with cling film, attached to the surface, and leave in the fridge until it sets to a jelly.

Transfer the jelly to a blender and blend on medium speed until you have a creamy, shiny gel. Transfer to a squeezy bottle and keep in the fridge for up to 10 days.

Make the spiced filo pastry: preheat the oven to 160°C fan (180°C), gas mark 4.

Place a sheet of baking paper (a little larger than the filo pastry sheet) on a clean work surface. Brush the paper with melted butter, then dust with icing sugar and place a sheet of filo pastry sheet on top. Brush the filo with melted butter, then sift with icing sugar and the ground cinnamon and cloves. Cover with another sheet of filo and repeat the

**GALAKTOBOUREKO CREAM:**

600ml full-fat milk
70ml double cream
80g fine semolina
130g caster sugar
180g eggs (3 large free-range eggs)
3 tsp vanilla extract with seeds
grated zest of ½ lemon
30g unsalted butter

**TO FINISH:**

a handful of fresh raspberries
a handful of fresh blackberries
a handful of fresh blueberries
40g raspberry pudding (*see page 244*)
10 mint leaves, thinly sliced
grated zest of ½ lime
icing sugar, for dusting

process until all the sheets are used. Brush the top sheet with melted butter and dust with icing sugar.

Cover with another sheet of baking paper and roll out with a rolling pin to make the filo sheets stick together and remove any trapped air. Remove the top sheet of baking paper. Take a 22–25cm cake ring (the same diameter as the serving bowl you plan to use) and place on top of the filo, then cut round it with a sharp knife.

Cover the filo disc again with baking paper and place on a baking tray. Place a weight on top (e.g. a pan filled with water or another tray) in order to keep the filo flat during baking. Bake in the preheated oven for 10–15 minutes, or until crisp. Remove from the oven and set aside to cool at room temperature.

Make the galaktoboureko cream (Thermomix method): put all the ingredients except the butter in a Thermomix bin and mix at 100°C, speed 5 for 20 minutes. Reduce the temperature to 37°C, add the butter and mix for 5 minutes. Strain into a container, cover with cling film, attached to the surface, and place in the fridge for 6 hours, or until cold and set. Using the paddle attachment on a food mixer, mix the cream for 2 minutes, to refresh it, and then transfer to a piping bag fitted with a star nozzle.

### ALTERNATIVELY (WITHOUT A THERMOMIX):

Make the galaktoboureko cream: heat the milk and cream in a saucepan set over a low heat until warmed through. In a bowl, whisk the semolina, sugar and eggs until well combined and then whisk in the warm milk and cream. Return to the pan and cook over a low heat, mixing with a whisk constantly, until the semolina is cooked and the mixture thickens – about 20–25 minutes. Remove from the heat and whisk in the vanilla extract and lemon zest, then transfer to blender. Blend on high speed for 10 minutes, or until the mixture is smooth, then gradually add the butter through the feed tube and mix for 3 minutes. Transfer to a container, cover with cling film, attached to the surface, and leave in the fridge for 6 hours, or until cold and set. Remove and whisk gently to refresh the cream, then transfer to a piping bag fitted with a star nozzle.

Assemble the dessert: pipe the galaktoboureko cream in 'star tips' over the base of a 22–25cm serving bowl. Scatter the berries over the cream, then squeeze out dots of the raspberry pudding in between the berries. Drizzle with the ginger syrup and garnish with mint and lime zest.

Cover the bowl with the spiced filo pastry disc and dust with icing sugar. When you're ready to serve, break the filo 'lid' with a spoon in front of your guests.

# SWEET TREATS
## A small taste of Greek hospitality

In the sun-kissed land of Greece, hospitality is not just a tradition; it's a way of life. From the moment you step foot into a Greek home, you are welcomed with open arms and treated like family. It's a warmth that emanates from the very soul of the Greek people, a generosity of spirit that knows no bounds.

Central to this tradition of hospitality is the concept of *kerasma* – the act of offering food and treats to guests as a gesture of friendship and goodwill. It's a tradition deeply rooted in our hearts, passed down through generations as a symbol of community. And nowhere is the spirit of *kerasma* more evident than in the realm of sweet treats. From delicate pastries to decadent desserts, Greek cuisine boasts a rich tapestry of sweets that are as diverse as the landscapes that shape the country.

In this way, sweet treats become more than just food; they are about sharing with others, a celebration of Greek hospitality that dictates that no guest should leave empty-handed. It's a tradition that speaks to the heart of what it means to be Greek – generous, welcoming and always ready to share the bounty of the table. So, as you indulge in the sweet delights of Greek cuisine, remember that in each bite of a Greek treat, you'll find the warmth of a welcoming smile, the embrace of a loving gesture, and the true essence of Greek hospitality.

# Olive Oil Macarons

Macarons nowadays come in so many flavours but have you ever tried an olive oil macaron? Our Greek version of the classic French treat. Easy to make while the trickiest part is to get the colour right.

**MAKES APPROX. 50 MACARONS**

- 250g icing sugar, sifted
- 250g ground almonds, sifted
- 1½ tsp water-soluble green food colouring powder (1.5g)
- 1 tsp water-soluble yellow food colouring powder (1g)
- ½ tsp water-soluble black food colouring powder (0.5g)
- 3 medium egg whites, left for 2 days in the fridge

**OLIVE OIL CREAM:**
- 200g white chocolate, cut into small pieces
- 100ml full-fat milk
- 100ml single cream
- 1 tbsp glucose syrup
- 65ml extra-virgin olive oil

**ITALIAN MERINGUE:**
- 250g caster sugar
- 60ml water
- 3 medium egg whites, left for 2 days in the fridge

Make the olive oil cream: melt the chocolate in the microwave or in a bowl suspended above a pan of simmering water, making sure the bottom of the bowl does not touch the water.

Warm the milk, cream and glucose syrup in a saucepan set over a medium heat and stir to combine. Remove from the heat and strain through a fine sieve over the melted chocolate. Gently fold them together with a rubber spatula and then transfer to a plastic jug. Slowly add the olive oil in a thin stream, mixing with a hand-held electric blender. The jug will help to keep the blender fully submerged and prevent air bubbles.

Transfer to a bowl and cover with cling film, attached to the surface. Leave to set in the fridge for 12 hours. Once set, whisk gently to refresh the cream, transfer to a piping bag and keep in the fridge until required.

Make the macarons: in a bowl, combine the sifted icing sugar, ground almonds and food colouring powders. Add the egg whites and mix well with a wooden spoon until everything combines to form a paste. Set aside.

Make the Italian meringue: put the sugar and water in a saucepan set over a medium heat. Bring to the boil, swirling the pan occasionally, and boil until the syrup becomes a caramel at 118°C (check with a sugar thermometer).

Meanwhile (before the sugar caramelizes), whisk the egg whites in a food mixer, fitted with the whisk attachment, until they form soft peaks. As soon as the caramel reaches 118°C, remove the pan from the heat and start pouring the caramel in a thin stream over the egg whites, whisking all the time until the mixture is glossy and the temperature has decreased to 45°C.

Add the meringue, in three batches, to the ground almond mixture, folding it in with a spatula until everything is thoroughly incorporated.

Transfer to a piping bag, fitted with a 10mm pastry nozzle, and pipe small circles, about 4cm in diameter, onto a baking sheet lined with baking paper (you can use silicone macaron mats with pre-marked circles, if wished), spacing them about 3cm apart. Tap the trays on the countertop to flatten and even out the piped mixture, then leave at room temperature for 1 hour, or until a skin forms on the surface of the meringues. This step is very important, as the skins will prevent the macarons from breaking during baking.

Preheat the oven to 160°C fan (180°C), gas mark 4.

Bake the macarons in the preheated oven for 8–10 minutes, or until they puff up by developing a smooth top with a wreath around it. Remove from the oven and leave at room temperature until completely cold before removing from the baking tray. They should lift off the baking paper easily without sticking and be chewy inside.

Pipe a small amount of olive oil cream onto the side of a macaron shell (the flat side that was touching the baking tray), leaving a small border around the edge. Cover with another shell, pressing down gently to create a macaron. Repeat with the remaining macarons and the olive oil cream. Place the macarons in a sealed container in the fridge for at least 6 hours before serving – this allows the texture to soften. Store in the fridge for up to 3 days.

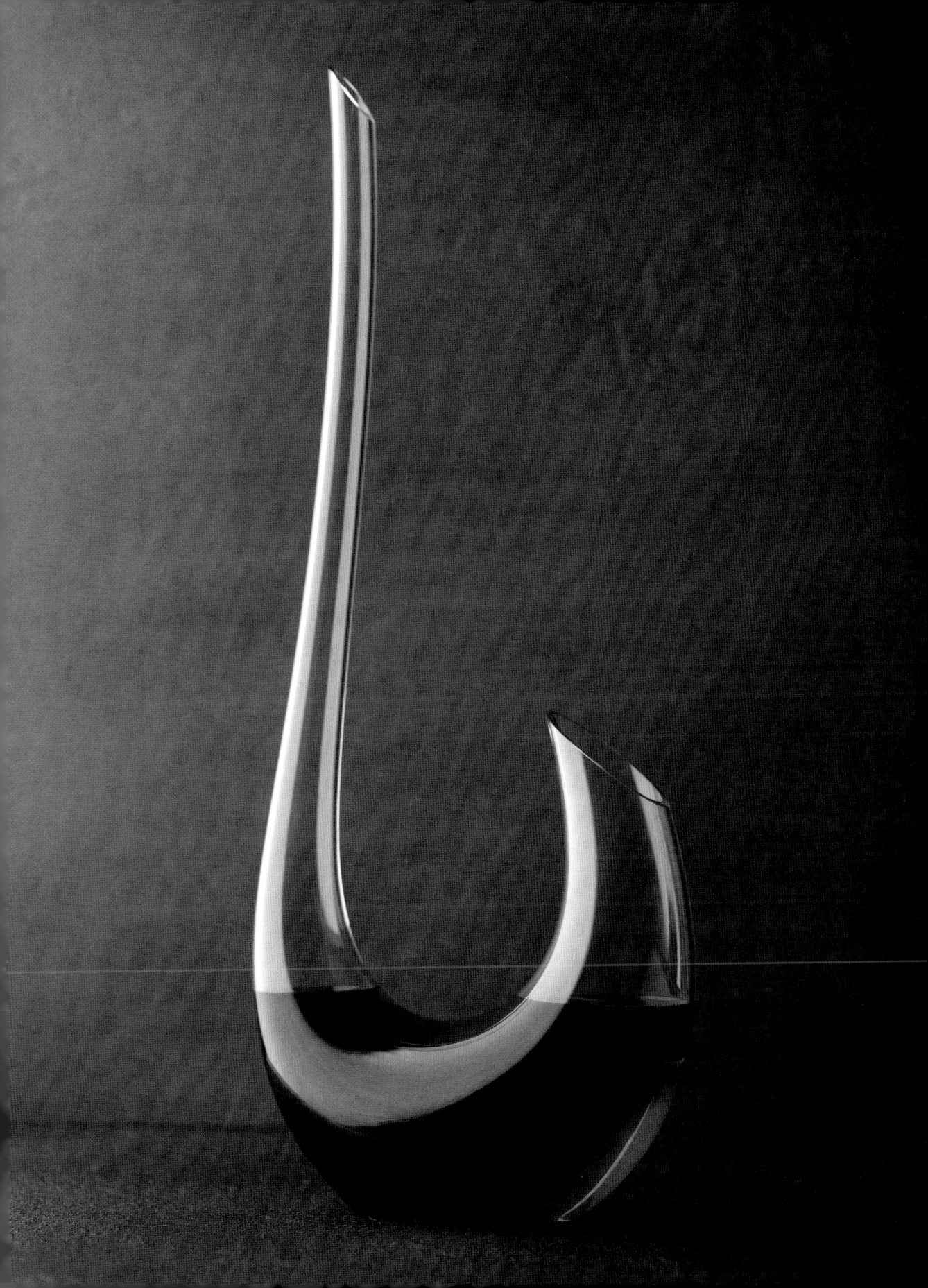

# Chocolate Mosaic

In Greek, this delicious sweet is known either as kormos, meaning a log, or as mosaiko, meaning mosaic. This is due to its log-shape, which, when sliced, reveals a marbled filling resembling a mosaic. Originally it was a quick dessert made by our mothers using cocoa, crumbled biscuits and Cognac. In this reimagined recipe, we substitute chocolate for cocoa powder to enhance the flavour, plus a secret ingredient – condensed milk – for an addictive chewy texture. The log is typically thin for small bites, but you can adjust its thickness when you roll it before freezing.

**MAKES 2 LOGS (APPROX. 10 SLICES PER LOG)**

50g dark chocolate (70% cocoa solids), chopped
60g unsalted butter, cubed
20g cocoa powder
100ml condensed milk
75g Lotus Biscoff biscuits, crumbled
50g pistachios, chopped
60g sour cherries in jam, strained and chopped

**DARK CHOCOLATE DECORATIONS (OPTIONAL):**
50g dark chocolate (70% cocoa solids), chopped
edible gold dust

**COCOA BUTTER COATING:**
100g dark chocolate (70% cocoa solids), chopped
100g cocoa butter, chopped

Make the dark chocolate decorations (if using): melt the chocolate in the microwave or in a bowl suspended above a pan of simmering water, without the bottom of the bowl touching the water.

Scrunch a large piece of baking paper to create creases all over it, then lay it flat on a tray. Using a spatula, spread the melted chocolate over the paper in a thin layer. Place in the freezer and leave until set and hard. Remove and brush the side of the chocolate that was touching the baking paper with some edible gold dust. Break into small pieces about 2cm square and transfer to a sealed container. Keep in the freezer until required.

Make the chocolate mosaic: melt the chocolate and the butter in the microwave or in a bowl suspended above a pan of simmering water, without the bottom of the bowl touching the water.

Put the cocoa powder and condensed milk in a bowl and stir in the melted chocolate-butter mixture, mixing with a rubber spatula until well combined. Add the crumbled Lotus biscuits, pistachios and sour cherries, then fold gently until incorporated. Divide the mixture into two equal-sized portions. Using a sheet of baking paper, roll each portion tightly into a 4cm diameter log and twist the ends to seal. Chill in the freezer.

Make the cocoa butter coating: melt the chocolate with the cocoa butter in the microwave or in a bowl suspended above a pan of simmering water, without the bottom of the bowl touching the water. Transfer to a plastic jug and mix with a hand-held electric blender until well combined. The jug will help to keep the blender fully submerged and prevent air bubbles. Transfer to a shallow container that is longer than the chocolate logs.

Remove the frozen chocolate logs from the freezer and unwrap them, discarding the baking paper. Dip them into the melted chocolate-cocoa butter mixture, turning them until they are completely coated. Place the coated logs on a tray lined with baking paper and chill in the fridge until the chocolate coating sets hard. Use any remaining chocolate-cocoa butter mixture as 'glue' to stick the chocolate decorations (if using) onto the log in the style of a mosaic.

Cut each log into 2cm-thick slices to serve. The logs will keep well in the fridge for up to 5 days.

# Melomakarona

These biscuits are the taste of Greek Christmas – the first sweet treats to appear at the beginning of the festive season in every Greek home and pastry shop. They are also the last ones to be removed from coffee tables and dining room consoles when Christmas and New Year are over.

**MAKES APPROX. 55 BISCUITS**

10g brown butter, melted (*see page 274*)
120ml sunflower oil
10g icing sugar
100ml fresh orange juice, strained
grated zest of 1 orange
300g plain flour, sifted
½ tsp bicarbonate of soda
½ tsp ground cinnamon
¼ tsp ground cloves
2 tbsp thyme honey, for drizzling

**HONEY SYRUP:**

200g caster sugar
40g thyme honey
peel of ½ orange
1 cinnamon stick
a pinch of ground cloves
280ml water

**CRUMBLE:**

40g walnuts, finely chopped
¼ tsp ground cinnamon
¼ tsp ground cloves

Make the honey syrup: put all the ingredients in a saucepan set over a medium heat and bring to the boil, stirring to dissolve the sugar. Remove from the heat and set aside to cool. Strain into a bowl or container, then cover and chill in the fridge. The syrup must be cold when used.

Preheat the oven to 180°C fan (200°C), gas mark 6. Line a baking tray with baking paper.

Put the melted brown butter, sunflower oil, icing sugar and orange juice and zest in a bowl. Whisk by hand until well combined.

In another bowl, mix the flour with the bicarbonate of soda, ground cinnamon and cloves. Make a well in the centre and pour in the orange juice mixture. Mix by hand until you have a soft dough – do not overwork the mixture.

Divide the dough into (approximately) 55 (10g) portions and shape into round balls. Place them on a large, lined baking tray, spacing them about 3cm apart, and gently press each one with the tines of a fork. Bake in the preheated oven for 25–35 minutes, or until crisp and cooked underneath.

Meanwhile, make the crumble: mix the walnuts, ground cinnamon and cloves in a bowl.

Remove the biscuits from the oven and, while they are hot, immerse them (in batches) in the chilled syrup for 1 minute. Remove with a slotted spoon and place on a wire rack. Drizzle with honey and sprinkle the crumble over the top. Set aside and when they are cold, store in an airtight container. They will keep well for up to 7 days.

# Chocolate Halvas

*Halvas* is commonly eaten during fasting periods because it is dairy-free. There are two different kinds of *halvas*: one is made with fine semolina and the other with tahini sesame paste. Even though we love the tahini *halvas*, our favourite is the semolina version. *Halvas* is a staple on 'Clean Monday', a festive day that marks the end of the carnival season (*Apokries*) and the beginning of the Great Lent before Orthodox Easter. It is customary on this day to fly kites and to picnic in the countryside with family and friends. *Halvas* has two really good friends: chocolate and citrus fruits!

**MAKES 35–40 CHOCOLATE HALVAS**

350g caster sugar
500ml water
2 cinnamon sticks
½ small tonka bean (optional), grated with a Microplane
100ml sunflower oil
200g fine semolina
finely grated zest of 1 orange

**CHOCOLATE PASTRY CREAM:**

130g dark chocolate (70% cocoa solids)
50g egg yolks (2 large egg yolks)
25g caster sugar
1 tbsp cornflour
190ml full-fat milk

**CHOCOLATE STICKS:**

50g dark chocolate (70% cocoa solids)

Make the chocolate pastry cream: melt the chocolate in the microwave or in a bowl suspended above a pan of simmering water (without the bowl touching the water). Remove from the heat and set aside while you make the chocolate pastry cream.

In a bowl, whisk the egg yolks, sugar and cornflour until well combined.

Warm the milk in a saucepan set over a low to medium heat and pour over the egg yolk mixture, whisking to incorporate. Return to the pan and set over a low heat. Whisk constantly until the mixture thickens. Remove from the heat and continue whisking for 1–2 minutes, to cook out the cornflour flavour.

Strain the mixture over the melted chocolate and whisk until well combined. Transfer to a bowl, then cover with cling film, attached to the surface, and leave to set in the fridge for 12 hours.

When the pastry cream is set, whisk gently to refresh it. Transfer to a piping bag with a star nozzle and keep in the fridge until required.

Make the halvas: put the sugar, water, cinnamon sticks and grated tonka (if using) in a saucepan. Set over a medium heat and bring to the boil, stirring to dissolve the sugar. Remove from the heat and strain through a sieve into a bowl. Keep it warm.

Heat the sunflower oil in a saucepan set over a medium heat and add the fine semolina. Cook, stirring continuously with a rubber spatula, until the semolina turns golden brown and gives off a nutty aroma. Reduce the heat to low and slowly pour in the warm sugar syrup, whisking continuously until the mixture thickens and becomes sandy (this takes 15–20 minutes). Take care as it will bubble and be very hot! The halvas is ready when it has a thick, pudding-like consistency and starts to pull away from the sides of the pan.

Pour the mixture onto a shallow tray lined with baking paper and set aside to cool at room temperature. Cover with cling film, attached to the surface of the halvas, and leave in the fridge until cold. Remove from the fridge and cut into bite-sized portions with a 4cm ring cutter, or into cubes using a knife.

Make the chocolate sticks: fill a large container with water and ice cubes. Melt the chocolate in the microwave or in a bowl suspended above a pan of simmering water (without the bowl touching the water). Transfer to a piping bag and cut the tip off the bag to create a 2mm hole. Pipe lines of chocolate straight into the iced water to create thin long sticks. Do not submerge the tip of the piping bag in the iced water, as this will chill the chocolate and block the piping bag hole. Leave them in the iced water for 15 minutes, then remove, pat dry and keep in the freezer. Once frozen, break the sticks into 2cm lengths.

To assemble the chocolate halvas, pipe a dot of chocolate pastry cream on top of each halvas disc or cube. Top with some dark chocolate sticks and sprinkle with grated orange zest.

SWEET TREATS

## Savoury

262 Chicken Stock
263 Fish Stock
264 Avgolemono Sauce
265 Béchamel Sauce
265 Lemon-Oregano Sauce
266 Chive Oil
266 Herb Oil
267 Chilli Oil
268 Smoked Tomato Sauce
269 Tomato Jam
270 Garlic Purée
270 Garlic Mayo
271 Confit of Shallots or Onions
271 Confit of Cherry Tomato
272 Basil Pesto
272 Chimichurri
273 Red Pepper Ketchup
273 Chilli Crunch
274 Brown Butter
274 Sherry Caramel Vinegar
275 Soya Caramel
275 Spice Rub

## Sweet

276 Simple Syrup
276 Hazelnut Crumble
277 Salted Caramel Cauce
277 Milk Chocolate Cream

# Basic Recipes

# Chicken Stock

**MAKES 1.5 LITRES**

2kg chicken wings
2 litres water
40g unsalted butter
1 red onion, sliced
1 leek, peeled and sliced
2 carrots, peeled and sliced
4 large garlic cloves, halved
250ml white wine
a handful of flat-leaf parsley sprigs
a few thyme sprigs

Place the chicken wings in a pressure cooker (without the lid) with the water, or enough to cover them. Bring to the boil, then cook for 10 minutes, skimming off any scum that rises to the surface.

Meanwhile, melt the butter in a saucepan set over a medium heat. Sweat the onion for 2 minutes, then add the leek and cook for 1–2 minutes. Add the carrots and cook for 2 minutes, then finally add the garlic and cook for 3–4 minutes.

Deglaze the pan with the white wine, scraping the bottom with a rubber spatula until the alcohol evaporates. Transfer the vegetables and their juices to the pressure cooker with the chicken wings and seal the lid.

Cook over a high heat until the pressure cooker starts to whistle. Reduce the heat to low and cook for 1 hour 30 minutes.

Remove from the heat and carefully release the trapped air. Leave for 10 minutes before opening the lid. Stir in the parsley and thyme and leave to steep for 30 minutes.

Strain the stock through a colander into a large container, discarding the chicken wings and vegetables. Strain again through cheesecloth (muslin) and store the strained stock in a container, covered with cling film, in the fridge for 1 day.

The following day, remove the fat from the surface of the stock with a spoon, and discard it. If wished, divide the stock between several zipper bags and keep them in the fridge for up to 1 week, or in the freezer for up to 1 month.

To use, transfer the desired quantity to a saucepan and bring to the boil.

# Fish Stock

**MAKES 600ML**

400g fish bones (including bones, head and/or tail)
2 tbsp extra-virgin olive oil
½ tomato, chopped
¼ red onion, chopped
½ celery stick, chopped
½ carrot, chopped
1 small garlic clove, crushed
750ml water
grated zest of ½ lemon
1 large thyme sprig
2 flat-leaf parsley sprigs

Rinse the fish bones thoroughly under cold running water and break the large ones into smaller pieces.

Heat the olive oil in a medium-sized saucepan and sauté the bones, head and tail over a high heat for 2–3 minutes. Add the tomato, red onion, celery, carrot and garlic and cook, stirring occasionally, for 2 minutes.

Add the water – there should be enough to just cover the bones – and bring to the boil. Reduce the heat to low and simmer for 20 minutes, skimming off any foamy scum and impurities on the surface with a ladle.

Remove the pan from the heat and stir in the lemon zest, thyme and parsley. Cover with cling film and set aside to steep for 10 minutes. Strain the stock through a colander lined with some cheesecloth (muslin) into a bowl. Discard the bones and vegetables.

Cover and cool down in the fridge. Use the same or the following day.

# Avgolemono Sauce

**MAKES 200ML**

3 tsp lemon juice, strained
a small handful of dill, chopped
½ tsp sea salt flakes
3–4 twists of freshly ground white pepper
2 medium free-range eggs
200ml chicken stock (see page 262), at room temperature or 200ml fish stock (see page 263), at room temperature

Put the lemon juice, dill, salt and pepper in a bowl and suspend it over a bowl of iced water.

Break the eggs into another bowl and whisk in the stock. Suspend the bowl over a pan of simmering water set over a medium heat, without the bottom of the bowl touching the water. Whisk constantly until the mixture amalgamates and becomes frothy (80°C on a sugar thermometer). Note: if you are using a Thermomix, set it to 80°C and mix at speed 6 for 8 minutes until frothy.

As soon as it reaches 80°C, strain the egg mixture through a sieve into the bowl of lemon juice and dill set over ice. Whisk constantly until the mixture cools down. Cover with cling film, attached to the surface, and set aside at room temperature until ready to serve.

Use the same day. Reheat carefully over a low heat, so it does not curdle.

**NOTE**: For meat recipes, such as the Giouvarlakia Dumplings (see page 92), use chicken stock.

For seafood recipes, such as the Grouper Avgolemono (see page 62) or the Monkfish Fricassee (see page 86), use fish stock.

# Béchamel Sauce

**MAKES 400ML**

500ml full-fat milk
2 tbsp chopped red onion
25g unsalted butter
25g plain flour, sifted
a pinch of fine salt
a pinch of ground nutmeg
15g graviera cheese, finely grated

Put the milk and onion in a saucepan set over a medium heat and warm gently. Remove from the heat and set aside, covered with cling film, for 30 minutes to infuse the milk with the flavour of the onion. Strain and discard the onion.

Melt the butter in another saucepan set over a medium heat and stir in the flour. Whisk constantly until you have a soft paste (*roux*). Cook gently for 1–2 minutes, or until it is lightly browned.

Add the strained milk and bring to the boil, whisking constantly and scraping the bottom of the pan, until the sauce thickens and coats the back of a spoon – it should be smooth, not lumpy. Remove from the heat and stir in the salt, nutmeg and graviera.

**TIP**: If lumpy, strain the sauce through a fine sieve.

# Lemon-Oregano Sauce

**MAKES 150ML**

600ml chicken stock (*see page 262*)
a knob of unsalted butter
2 tsp lemon juice, strained
3 twists of freshly ground white pepper
a pinch of sea salt flakes
a pinch of dried oregano

Put the chicken stock in a saucepan and cook over a medium to high heat until it reduces to approximately 150ml and has the consistency of a glaze. Add the butter and cook for a few minutes until incorporated.

Remove from the heat and stir in the lemon juice, pepper, salt and oregano. Use the sauce immediately.

# Chive Oil

**MAKES 200ML**

200ml extra-virgin olive oil
a bunch of chives, chopped
½ garlic clove, crushed
a pinch of fine salt

Blitz all the ingredients in a blender until incorporated.

Place a strainer lined with cheesecloth (muslin) over a bowl. Pour the chive mixture into the strainer and leave it in the fridge for at least 2 hours to strain, without applying any pressure.

Transfer the strained chive oil to a squeezy bottle and keep in the fridge for up to 4 days.

# Herb Oil

**MAKES 200ML**

200ml extra-virgin olive oil
a small bunch of thyme sprigs
2 rosemary sprigs
1 garlic clove, crushed
a few whole black peppercorns

Put all the ingredients in a saucepan and set over a low to medium heat. Gently warm for a few minutes – do not overheat nor allow the mixture to simmer or boil.

Remove from the heat, cover with clingfilm and leave to steep for 2 hours. Strain through cheesecloth (muslin) into a bowl, then transfer to a squeezy bottle and keep in the fridge for up to 1 week.

# Chilli Oil

**MAKES 250ML**

30g long red chilli peppers
a pinch of fine salt
250ml extra-virgin olive oil, plus extra for drizzling
170g roasted red peppers in brine, drained

Preheat the oven to 180°C fan (200°C), gas mark 6. Line a baking tray with baking paper.

Place the chillies on the lined baking tray. Season with salt and drizzle with olive oil. Bake in the preheated oven for 15 minutes.

Remove from the oven and set aside until cool. Discard the stems and place the chillies in a blender with the olive oil and roasted red peppers. Blitz until well combined.

Place a strainer lined with cheesecloth (muslin) over a bowl. Pour the mixture into the strainer and leave it in the fridge overnight to strain, without applying any pressure.

The following day, transfer the strained oil to a piping bag and seal. Let it hang for at least 3 hours at room temperature, or until the water separates from the oil and sits at the bottom of the piping bag. Punch a small hole at the bottom of the bag and discard the water.

Transfer the chilli oil to a squeezy bottle and keep in the fridge for up to 7 days.

# Smoked Tomato Sauce

For the smoking process you will need two metal containers: a deep one plus a shallow perforated container that fits on top of the deep container.

**MAKES 500G**

1kg ripe and juicy San Marzano tomatoes
½ cup oak wood chips
100ml extra-virgin olive oil
1 small red onion, finely diced
1 small garlic clove, finely chopped
2 tbsp caster sugar
1 tsp fine salt

With a knife, remove the core of each tomato and score an 'X' at the bottom.

Blanch the tomatoes in a saucepan of boiling water for 10 seconds and then plunge them into a bowl of iced water. Remove the tomatoes with a slotted spoon and peel away the skins.

Transfer the skinned tomatoes to the perforated shallow metal container. Place the oak wood chips in the deep metal container and light them with a blowtorch. As soon as they are alight, glowing and releasing smoke, quickly place the perforated container with the tomatoes on top and seal both containers with kitchen foil to trap the smoke. Leave the tomatoes to smoke for 20–25 minutes.

Remove the tomatoes from the metal container, then cut them in half and scoop out and discard the seeds. Place the tomato flesh in a blender and blitz until you have a smooth purée.

Heat the olive oil in a saucepan set over a medium heat and sauté the onion, stirring occasionally, for 3–4 minutes, or until softened. Add the garlic and cook for 1 minute.

Stir in the smoked tomato purée, sugar and salt and cook gently over a low to medium heat, stirring occasionally, for 30 minutes, or until you have a thick, flavoursome sauce. Remove from the heat and set aside at room temperature to cool down. Use the same or the following day.

# Tomato Jam

**MAKES 500G**

1kg ripe and juicy San Marzano tomatoes
100ml extra-virgin olive oil
1 small red onion, finely diced
1 small garlic clove, finely chopped
2 tbsp caster sugar
1 tsp fine salt

With a sharp knife, remove the core of each tomato, then cut in half and scrape out and discard the seeds. Coarsely grate the tomatoes and discard the skin.

Heat the olive oil in a saucepan set over a medium heat and sauté the onion, stirring occasionally, for 3–4 minutes, or until softened. Add the garlic and cook for 1 minute. Add the grated tomatoes and their juice, together with the sugar and salt, and cook over a low to medium heat, stirring occasionally, for approximately 30 minutes, or until you have a thick, flavoursome sauce.

Remove from the heat and set aside at room temperature to cool down. Use the same or the following day.

# Garlic Purée

**MAKES 200–250G**

10 whole garlic heads, halved
7 tbsp extra-virgin olive oil
sea salt flakes
20 small thyme sprigs

Preheat the oven to 180°C fan (200°C), gas mark 6.

For every garlic half, cut a piece of kitchen foil that is large enough to wrap it.

Place each garlic half on a piece of foil and sprinkle with 1 teaspoon olive oil, a mere pinch of sea salt and a small sprig of thyme.

Wrap each garlic half individually in the foil and place on a baking tray. Bake in the preheated oven for 45–50 minutes, or until soft. Take the tray out of the oven and leave until the garlic is cool enough to handle.

Unwrap the foil, discard the thyme and press to squeeze out the garlic flesh (discarding the skins) into a blender.

Blend until creamy and keep in an airtight container in the fridge for up to 15 days.

# Garlic Mayo

**MAKES 500G**

50g garlic purée (*see above*)
2 tbsp simple syrup (*see page 276*)
4 tsp sherry vinegar
2 medium free-range egg yolks
1 tsp fine salt
500ml sunflower oil

Put all the ingredients except the sunflower oil in a bowl and whisk until well combined.

Start adding the sunflower oil steadily in a thin stream, whisking constantly until well incorporated and you have a thick and creamy mayonnaise.

Store in a sealed container in the fridge for up to 15 days.

# Confit of Shallots or Onions

**MAKES 8 CONFIT BANANA SHALLOTS**
*OR* **20 CONFIT SMALL SHALLOTS**
*OR* **40 CONFIT PEARL ONIONS**

4 banana shallots *or* 10 small shallots *or* 20 pearl onions
120ml extra-virgin olive oil
60ml sherry vinegar
2 tbsp caster sugar
2 tsp allspice berries
1 cinnamon stick
2 large thyme sprigs

Preheat the oven to 180°C fan (200°C), gas mark 6. Line a baking tray with baking paper.

Cut the shallots or onions in half lengthwise, leaving the skins on. Place them, skin-side up, on the lined baking tray. Drizzle with olive oil and sherry vinegar, then sprinkle with the sugar and allspice berries. Tuck in the cinnamon stick and thyme, then cover with kitchen foil.

Bake in the preheated oven for 30 minutes. Remove the foil and cook for 10 more minutes. Remove from the oven and set aside to cool before discarding the skins together with the herbs and spices. Use the same day.

# Confit of Cherry Tomatoes

**MAKES 20 CONFIT CHERRY TOMATOES**

10 cherry tomatoes, halved
3 tbsp extra-virgin olive oil
a pinch of fine salt
1 tsp caster sugar
3–4 twists of freshly ground white pepper
1 small garlic clove, thinly sliced
1 thyme sprig
1 rosemary sprig

Preheat the oven to 180°C fan (200°C), gas mark 6. Line a small baking tray with baking paper.

Place the tomatoes on the lined baking tray. Drizzle with olive oil and sprinkle with fine salt, sugar and pepper. Tuck in the garlic and herbs and cover with kitchen foil.

Bake in the preheated oven for 12 minutes, then remove the foil and bake for 3 more minutes. Remove from the oven and set aside to cool down. Discard the herbs and garlic. Use the same day.

# Basil Pesto

**MAKES 250G**

35g graviera cheese, finely grated
100g pine nuts
a pinch of sea salt flakes
2–3 twists of freshly ground white pepper
40g basil leaves
25g mascarpone cheese
70ml extra-virgin olive oil, plus extra for preserving the pesto

Put all the ingredients in a blender and blitz for a few seconds. Scrape down the sides of the blender continuously until you have a smooth mixture.

Transfer to a container, then drizzle with enough olive oil to cover the surface of the pesto and preserve its bright green colour. Cover with a lid and keep in the fridge for up to 3 days.

# Chimichurri

**MAKES 300G**

1 tsp cardamom seeds
2 tsp coriander seeds
½ tsp cumin seeds
1 tsp whole Madagascar peppercorns
90g green chillies, finely chopped
½ garlic clove, finely chopped
30g flat-leaf parsley leaves, roughly chopped
30g coriander leaves, roughly chopped
2 tsp lemon juice, strained
180ml extra-virgin olive oil

In a saucepan set over a medium heat, toast the seeds and peppercorns for 1–2 minutes, tossing gently until they release their aroma. Remove from the heat and crush them with a pestle and mortar or in a spice grinder. (Alternatively, grind in a pepper mill.)

Transfer to a blender and blitz with the chillies, garlic, herbs, lemon juice and half the olive oil. With the motor running, slowly add the remaining olive oil in a thin stream through the feed tube until well incorporated.

Transfer to a container and cover with cling film, attached to the surface. Cover and keep in the fridge for up to 4 days.

# Red Pepper Ketchup

**MAKES 350G**

4 tsp extra-virgin olive oil
1 shallot, thinly sliced
50g soft light brown sugar
250g roasted red peppers in brine, strained
200g chopped tomatoes
50ml water
40ml rice vinegar
a generous pinch of sweet and smoked paprika
a pinch of fine salt
a pinch of ground cumin
½ star anise

Heat the olive oil in a saucepan set over a low heat and sauté the shallot, stirring occasionally, for 4–5 minutes, or until softened. Stir in the brown sugar and cook for 1 minute.

Add the remaining ingredients and cover the pan with a lid. Simmer gently for 35–40 minutes, or until most of the juices have evaporated.

Remove from the heat, discard the star anise and transfer to a blender. Pulse until you have a smooth sauce.

Strain through a fine sieve into a container and leave to cool at room temperature. Transfer to a squeezy bottle and keep in the fridge for up to 7 days.

# Chilli Crunch

**MAKES 140G**

100g red chilli peppers
40ml extra-virgin olive oil

Chargrill the red chilli peppers over charcoal or on a cast iron skillet set over a medium heat. Cook them, turning occasionally, until lightly charred all over. Transfer to a tray and set aside to cool.

When cold, remove and discard the stems. Finely chop the charred chilli peppers and transfer to a container. Add the olive oil and stir gently. Cover with a lid and keep in the fridge for up to 7 days.

# Brown Butter

**MAKES 70G**

100g unsalted butter

Put the butter in a saucepan set over a medium heat. Cook, swirling the pan constantly, until the butter melts and turns brown with a nutty aroma.

Strain immediately through cheesecloth (muslin) into a container and keep in the fridge for up to 5 days.

**NOTE**: If you're making a bigger quantity, use a sugar thermometer to measure the temperature, and cook the butter, swirling it, until it reaches 155°C.

# Sherry Caramel Vinegar

**MAKES 100ML**

150ml sherry vinegar
90ml water
80g caster sugar

Put all the ingredients in a saucepan set over a medium heat. Bring to the boil and stir to dissolve the sugar.

Reduce the heat to low and simmer gently for 20 minutes, or until the liquid reduces to approximately 100ml and has a syrupy consistency.

Transfer to a squeezy bottle and keep in the fridge for up to 7 days.

# Soya Caramel

**MAKES 60ML**

100ml light soy sauce (reduced salt)
100g caster sugar

Put the soy sauce and sugar in a saucepan set over a low to medium heat. Simmer gently, stirring occasionally, until the sugar dissolves and the mixture reduces and caramelizes at 105°C (you can measure this with a sugar thermometer).

Remove from the heat and leave to cool at room temperature.

Transfer to a squeezy bottle or a sealed container and keep in the fridge for up to 7 days.

# Spice Rub

**MAKES 55G**

3 tsp garlic powder
2 tsp dried oregano
4 tsp fine salt
1½ tsp smoked paprika
½ tsp freshly ground white pepper
¼ tsp chilli powder
a pinch of onion powder

Mix all the ingredients together in a bowl.

Transfer to a sealed container and store at room temperature for up to 15 days.

# Simple Syrup

**MAKES 120ML**

100ml water
100g caster sugar

Put the water and sugar in a saucepan and set over a medium heat. Bring to the boil, swirling the pan occasionally until the sugar dissolves.

Remove from heat and leave to cool at room temperature. Once cold, transfer to a squeezy bottle and keep in the fridge for up to 7 days.

# Hazelnut Crumble

**MAKES 500G**

100g unsalted butter, cubed
100g soft light brown sugar
30g caster sugar
1 tsp vanilla extract with seeds
1 tsp ground cinnamon
a pinch of ground nutmeg
100g plain flour, sifted
180g roasted hazelnuts, roughly chopped

Using the paddle attachment on a food mixer, mix the butter and sugars until creamy. Add the vanilla extract and mix for 1 minute. Add the cinnamon, nutmeg and flour, and mix well. Add the chopped hazelnuts and mix again until everything is well combined.

Remove the dough and, on a clean work surface, knead gently by hand into a ball. Wrap the dough in cling film and leave in the freezer until frozen.

Preheat the oven to 180°C fan (200°C), gas mark 6. Line a baking tray with baking paper.

Remove the dough from the freezer and leave at room temperature for 5–10 minutes to soften it a little. Coarsely grate it onto the lined baking tray, spreading it out evenly. Make sure that each time you pass it through the grater, you grate it with a long continuous movement, so the crumble is as big as possible.

Bake in the preheated oven for 5–6 minutes, or until golden brown. Remove from the oven and leave to cool at room temperature. Break it into chunky pieces by hand, if needed.

Store in a sealed container at room temperature for up to 3 days.

# Salted Caramel Sauce

**MAKES 150G**

100ml single cream
20ml water
80g caster sugar
½ tsp sea salt flakes
65g milk chocolate (40% cocoa solids), melted
55g unsalted butter

Warm the cream in a saucepan set over a low heat.

Put the water and sugar in another pan and bring to a simmer. Cook gently until the syrup turns to a caramel consistency with a light amber colour and reaches 180°C on a sugar thermometer.

Carefully, stir in the warm cream, whisking constantly, until well combined and the bubbling has almost stopped. Add the sea salt and melted chocolate and mix until smooth.

Transfer the mixture to a small plastic jug, add the butter and mix with a hand-held electric blender until well combined and smooth. The jug will help to keep the blender fully submerged in the mixture and will prevent air bubbles.

Transfer the sauce to a container, lay some cling film on the surface and leave to cool down at room temperature. Transfer to a squeezy bottle and keep in the fridge for up to 3 days. Before using, remove from the fridge for a couple of hours until it softens and reaches a pourable consistency, similar to caramel.

# Milk Chocolate Cream

**MAKES 500G**

3g gelatine sheets
100ml full-fat milk
5g glucose syrup
200g milk chocolate (40% cocoa solids), melted
200ml double cream

Soak the gelatine sheets in a bowl of iced water until softened.

Warm the milk and glucose in a saucepan set over a low heat. Gently squeeze any water out of the softened gelatine and add to the pan, whisking until the gelatine dissolves.

Strain the warm milk mixture into the melted chocolate and mix gently with a rubber spatula until well combined.

Transfer the mixture to a plastic jug and mix with a hand-held electric blender, adding the double cream, until well combined and shiny – the jug will help to keep the blender fully submerged in the mixture and will prevent air bubbles.

Transfer to a bowl, cover with cling film, attached to the surface, and leave in the fridge for at least 12 hours until set. Once set, whisk gently to refresh the cream, then transfer to a piping bag and keep in the fridge for up to 5 days.

# INDEX

Note: page numbers in **bold** refer to illustrations.

## A

almond
  almond cream 210–11
  chocolate tarts 240–2
  extra-virgin olive oil parfait 236
  olive oil macarons 250–1
Amaretto pudding 224–6
apple crumble Greek toast 165, **166**
aubergine
  aubergine imam 122, **123**
  aubergine mash 102–3, **103**
  moussakas 95
  sea bass imam 58
avgolemono sauce 40–1, **41**, 264
  fricassee sauce 86
  giouvarlakia dumplings 92
  grouper avgolemono 62, **63**
avocado
  avocado mash 178, **179**
  kale & feta bowl 192
  spicy chicken bowl 188

## B

*bakaliko* (neighbourhood grocery shop) 16, 76
baking 194–217
balsamic dressing 36, **37**
banana
  Greek yoghurt with tahini & banana topping 157, **159**
  Lotus crumble 162, **163**
  peanut butter & banana Greek toast 165, **167**
barbecue 106–48
barley 78, **79**
basil
  basil pesto 80, **81**, 116, 272
  prawns mikrolimano 60
  tomato basil salsa 116, **117**
  tuna parmesan 80
bean(s)
  black-eyed beans 82, **83**
  charred long beans 126, **127**
  fava 22, **23**
  tuna bowl 190
béchamel sauce 95, 102–3, 265

beef 128
  beef cheeks giouvetsi 96–7, **97**
  beef shank hunkiar 102–3, **103**
  coffee beef picanha 142, **143**
  moussakas 95, **95**
  souvlaki 136, **137**
  ultimate burgers 138, **139**
beetroot salad 44–5, **45**
biscuits
  melomakarona 256, **257**
  see also cookies
black-eyed bean(s) 82, **83**
blackberry
  berry topping 157, **158**
  galaktoboureko 244–6, **245**, **247**
  pickled blackberries 44–5, **45**
  rizogalo brûlée 168
  very berry pancake topping 160, **161**
blueberry
  berry topping 157, **158**
  galaktoboureko 244–6, **245**, **247**
  granola topping 156
  Greek yoghurt & toppings 156–7
  rizogalo brûlée 168
  very berry pancake topping 160, **161**
bottarga
  skate wing bottarga 84, **85**
  taramas 20
bowls 186–92
  kale & feta bowl 192, **193**
  spicy chicken bowl 188, **189**
  tuna bowl 190, **191**
bread 196–203
  flatbreads 132, **133**, 136, **137**
  hot dog buns 200
  koulouri bread 174, 176, 198, **199**, **201**
  pitta flatbreads 120, **121**, 182, **183**, 214, **215**
  tsoureki 216–17, **217**
  see also brioche; sourdough bread
breakfast 154–68
brioche
  Greek toast 164–5, **166–7**
  tahini brioche 138, **139**, 208–9, **209**
  tsoureki 216–17, **217**
broccoli, smoked broccoli 42, **43**
brûlée, rizogalo brûlée 168, **169**
brunch 150–92
burgers, ultimate burgers 138, **139**
butter
  brown butter 256, 274
  curry butter 46, **47**

## C

cakes, vasilopita (New Year's cake) 206, **207**
capers
  Dakos salad 36
  fried capers 66–7, **67**
  octopus stifado 82
  skate wing bottarga 84
  tartare sauce 138
caramel
  caramelized hazelnuts 165, **167**
  soya caramel 188, 275
  see also salted caramel sauce
carbonara, eel carbonara 76, **77**
carpaccio
  Greek salad carpaccio 68, **69**
  ox tongue carpaccio 24, **25**
carrot 74, 86, 262–3
catch of the day crudo 64, **65**
caul fat, veal liver in caul fat 140
cauliflower, roasted cauliflower 46, **47**
caviar (Ossetra), squid matsata 70
charcoaled meat 128–42
charcoaled turbot 146, **147**
chard
  charred greens 62, **63**
  fish & greens 148
  village eggs 172
cheese
  Metsovone croquette 26, **27**
  tuna parmesan 80, **81**
  ultimate burgers 138, **139**
  see also cream cheese; feta cheese; goat's curd cheese; graviera cheese; mascarpone cheese
cheesecake, baked feta cheesecake 238, **239**
cherry
  baked feta cheesecake 238
  cherry soup 236, **237**
  chocolate mosaic 254–5
  extra-virgin olive oil parfait 236
  sour cherry & lime topping 157, **158**
chicken
  chicken okra 104, **105**
  lemon oregano chicken 100, **101**
  spicy chicken bowl 188, **189**
  see also chicken stock
chicken stock 262
  avgolemono sauce 40–1, 264
  beef cheeks giouvetsi 96–7
  lamb shank trahanas 98–9
  lemon-oregano sauce 265

278  Index

moussakas 95
smoked tomato lobster 78
spinach rice pilaf 48
chilli crunch 114, 188, 273
chilli oil 60, 267
chilli powder 92, 130, 132, 182, 275
chimichurri 272
dolmades 112
lamb & eel kebabs 130
tuna bowl 190
chips
potato chips 95, **95**
salsify chips 96-7
chive oil 266
charred lettuce 38
chicken okra 104
giouvarlakia dumplings 92
stuffed courgettes 40-1
chives 48, 66-7, 76, 98-9, 172, 180, 182
chocolate
chocolate halvas 258-9, **259**
chocolate mosaic 254-5, **255**
chocolate pastry cream 258-9, **259**
chocolate sticks 258-9, **259**
chocolate tarts 240-2, **243**
cocoa craquelin 224-6, **227**
extra-virgin olive oil parfait 236
Greek yoghurt & toppings 156-7
Lotus crumble 162, **163**
milk chocolate cream 216-17, **217**, 224-6, **227**, 277
milk chocolate tonka cream 241, **243**
moustokoulouro Alaska & sandwich 232-4
peanut butter & banana Greek toast 165, **167**
peanut butter chocolate crumble 162, **163**
salted caramel sauce 277
see also white chocolate
choux pastry, Greek coffee tiramisu profiteroles 224-6, **227**
cinnamon
apple crumble Greek toast 165
chocolate halvas 258-9
cinnamon rolls 210-11, **212-13**
confit of shallots or onions 271
ginger syrup 244-6
Greek yoghurt with tahini & banana topping 157
hazelnut crumble 156, 276
melomakarona 256
moussakas 95
moustokoulouro Alaska & sandwich 232-4

poached quinces 242
rizogalo brûlée 168
spiced filo pastry 244-6
vasilopita (New Year's cake) 206
citrus curd 228, **229**
cloves 182, 206, 232-4, 242, 244-6, 256
cocoa butter coating 254-5, **255**
cocoa craquelin 224-6, **227**
coffee
coffee beef picanha 142, **143**
coffee crumble 225-6, **227**
coffee rub 142, **143**
Greek coffee tiramisu profiteroles 222, 224-6, **227**
moustokoulouro Alaska & sandwich 232-4
confit of cherry tomato 271
charcoaled turbot 146
charred long beans 126
green kayanas 178
confit of egg yolk 66-7, **67**, 76, **77**
confit of pearl onion 146, 184, 271
confit of shallot 82, 104, 271
cookies, moustokoulouro Alaska & sandwich 232-4, **233**, **235**
coriander leaf 178, 272
tomato & coriander salsa 24, **25**, 192, **193**
courgette, stuffed courgettes 40-1, **41**
craquelin
cocoa craquelin 224-6, **227**
'tiger' craquelin 202-3
cream
almond cream 210-11
chocolate pastry cream 258-9, **259**
extra-virgin olive oil parfait 236, **237**
galaktoboureko cream **245**, 246, **247**
mascarpone coffee cream 224-6, **227**
milk chocolate cream 224-6, **227**, 277
milk chocolate tonka cream 241, **243**
olive oil cream 250-1, **252**
tsoureki 216-17, **217**
vanilla cream 228, **229**
white chocolate & cheese cream 242
cream cheese
baked feta cheesecake 238, **239**
white chocolate & cheese cream 242

crème Anglaise 164
croquette, Metsovone croquette 26, **27**
crumble 256, **257**
apple crumble Greek toast 165, **166**
coffee crumble 225-6, **227**
hazelnut crumble 156, 242, 276
Lotus crumble 162, **163**
peanut butter chocolate crumble 162, **163**
cumin 138, 142, 272, 273
cumin yoghurt 182, **183**
curd, citrus curd 228, **229**
curing 56
curry butter 46, **47**
curry mayo 46, **47**

# D

Dakos salad 36, **37**
desserts 222-46
dill 18, 40-1, 48, 86, 92, 130, 264
dips, lemon yoghurt dip 30-1, **31**
dolmades 112, **113**
'dough window effect' 211
dressings, balsamic dressing 36, **37**
dumplings, giouvarlakia dumplings 92, **93**

# E

edible flowers 48, 62
eel
eel carbonara 76, **77**
lamb & eel kebabs 130, **131**
egg(s) 170-84
almond cream 210-11
avgolemono sauce 40-1, 264
baked feta cheesecake 238
chocolate pastry cream 258-9
chocolate tarts 240-2
cinnamon rolls 210-11
citrus curd 228
crème Anglaise 164
eel carbonara 76
egg wash 217
egg yolk confit 66-7, **67**, 76, **77**
eggs saganaki 184, **185**
feta kataifi 28
galaktoboureko cream 246
garlic mayo 270
giouvarlakia dumplings 92
Greek eggs Benedict & royale 174-6, **175**, **177**
Greek yoghurt hollandaise 174
green kayanas 178
kale & feta bowl 192
lamb & eel kebabs 130

mascarpone coffee cream 224–6
Metsovone croquette 26
mountain eggs 180, **181**
moustokoulouro Alaska & sandwich 232–4
olive oil macarons 250–1
open pitta lamb 182
pancakes 160
pâté brisée 30–1
rizogalo brûlée 168
spanakopita 30–1
spicy chicken bowl 188
strawberry pavlova 228–30
tahini brioche 208–9
tsoureki 216–17
vanilla cream 228
vasilopita (New Year's cake) 206
village eggs 172, **173**

# F

fava 22, **23**
feta cheese
  aubergine imam 122
  baked feta cheesecake 238, **239**
  charred lettuce 38
  charred long beans 126
  Dakos salad 36
  eggs saganaki 184
  feta kataifi 28, **29**
  Greek salad carpaccio 68
  green kayanas 178
  grilled feta 114, **115**
  kale & feta bowl 192, **193**
  lemon oregano chicken 100
  prawns mikrolimano 60
  smoked potato salad 124
  spanakopita 30–1
  spinach rice pilaf 48
filo pastry
  feta kataifi 28, **29**
  galaktoboureko 244–6, **245**, **247**
fish
  barbecued whole fish 144–8
  catch of the day crudo 64, **65**
  charcoaled turbot 146, **147**
  fish & greens 148, **149**
  fish marinade 74, **75**
  fish stock 263
  Greek eggs royale 176
  Greek salad carpaccio 68, **69**
  grouper avgolemono 62, **63**
  kakavia fishermen's soup 74, **75**
  monkfish fricassee 86, **87**
  red mullet pitta wraps 120, **121**
  sea bass imam 58, **59**
  skate wing bottarga 84, **85**

stuffed courgettes 40–1, **41**
tuna ladolemono 66–7, **67**
tuna parmesan 80, **81**
flatbreads
  DIY gyros wraps 132, **133**
  olive oil flatbreads 120, **121**
  souvlaki 136, **137**
fricassee sauce 86, **87**

# G

galaktoboureko 244–6, **245**, **247**
garlic mayo 46, 174, 270
garlic purée 270
  curry butter 46
  garlic mayo 270
  garlic soup 70
  lemon yoghurt dip 30–1
  tzatziki 18
garlic soup 70, **71**
gelatine 224–6, 228, 241–2, 277
gherkin(s)
  smoked potato salad 124
  tartare sauce 138
  ultimate burgers 138
ginger syrup 244–6
giouvarlakia dumplings 92, **93**
giouvetsi, beef cheeks giouvetsi 96–7, **97**
goats 90, 128
goat's curd cheese
  spinach rice pilaf 48, **49**
  village eggs 172
gold leaf (edible) 206, 236
granola topping 156
graviera cheese
  basil pesto 80, 272
  béchamel sauce 95, 102–3, 265
  eel carbonara 76
  lamb shank trahanas 98–9
  moussakas 95
  panko mixture 46
  smoked tomato lobster 78
  tuna parmesan 80
Greek yoghurt
  berry topping 157
  cumin yoghurt 182, **183**
  curry mayo 46
  giouvarlakia dumplings 92
  Greek yoghurt & toppings 156–7, **158–9**
  Greek yoghurt hollandaise 174, 176
  Greek yoghurt with tahini & banana topping 157, **159**
  Greek yoghurt wasabi 42, **43**
  lamb & eel kebabs 130
  lemon yoghurt dip 30–1, **31**
  red mullet pitta wraps 120

sea bass imam 58
smoked yoghurt 172, **173**
sour cherry & lime topping 157
tartare sauce 138
tzatziki 18
vasilopita (New Year's cake) 206
greens
  charred greens 62, **63**
  fish & greens 148, **149**
  village eggs 172
grouper avgolemono 62, **63**
gyros, DIY gyros wraps 132, **133**

# H

halvas, chocolate halvas 258–9, **259**
hazelnut
  caramelized hazelnuts 165, **167**
  granola topping 156
  hazelnut crumble 156, 242, 276
  hazelnut streusel 165, **166**
  panko mixture 46
herb oil 42, 266
hollandaise, Greek yoghurt hollandaise 174, 176
honey (thyme) 28, 36, 208–9
  Greek yoghurt & toppings 156–7
  Greek yoghurt with tahini & banana topping 157
  honey syrup 210–11, 256
  melomakarona 256
  moustokoulouro Alaska & sandwich 232–4
  poached quinces 242
hot dog buns 200
hunkiar, beef shank hunkiar 102–3, **103**

# I

ice cream
  apple crumble Greek toast 165, **166**
  moustokoulouro Alaska & sandwich 232–4, **233**, **235**
  peanut butter & banana Greek toast 165, **167**
Italian meringue 234, **235**, 250–1, **252**

# J

jams
  rhubarb jam 26, **27**
  strawberry jam 157, **158**, 160
  tomato jam 80, 96–7, 269

## K

kakavia fishermen's soup 74, **75**
kale
    Greek eggs royale 176
    kale & feta bowl 192, **193**
kataifi filo pastry, feta kataifi 28, **29**
kayanas, green kayanas 178, **179**
kebabs, lamb & eel kebabs 130, **131**
*kerasma* concept 248
ketchup, red pepper ketchup 273
koulouri bread 174, 176, 198, **199**, **201**

## L

ladolemono, tuna ladolemono 66-7, **67**
lamb 90, 128
    giouvarlakia dumplings 92, **93**
    lamb & eel kebabs 130, **131**
    lamb shank trahanas 98-9, **99**
    open pitta lamb 182, **183**
lemon
    avgolemono sauce 40-1, 62, 86, 92, 264
    citrus curd 228, **229**
    lemon yoghurt dip 30-1, **31**
    lemon-oregano sauce 100, 104, 265
lettuce
    charred lettuce 38, **39**
    fricassee sauce 86
    grilled baby gem 100, **101**
    octopus dog 118
levain starter 202-3
lime
    citrus curd 228, **229**
    sour cherry & lime topping 157, **158**
liver, veal liver in caul fat 140, **141**
lobster, smoked tomato lobster 78, **79**
Lotus Biscoff biscuits
    chocolate mosaic 254-5
    Lotus crumble/sauce 162, **163**

## M

macarons, olive oil macarons 250-1, **252-3**
marinades, fish marinade 74, **75**
mascarpone cheese
    basil pesto 80, 272
    mascarpone coffee cream 224-6, **227**
    very berry pancake topping 160
mash
    aubergine mash 102-3, **103**
    avocado mash 178, **179**
    mashed potato 100, **101**
matsata, squid matsata 70, **71**
mayonnaise
    curry mayo 46, **47**
    garlic mayo 46, 174, 270
    tartare sauce 138
meat 88-104
    charcoaled meat 128-42
Mediterranean diet 34, 52
melomakarona 256, **257**
meringue
    moustokoulouro Alaska & sandwich 232-4, **233**, **235**
    olive oil macarons 250-1, **252**
    strawberry pavlova 228-30, **229**, **231**
Metsovone croquette 26, **27**
monkfish fricassee 86, **87**
moussakas 95, **95**
moustokoulouro Alaska & sandwich 232-4, **233**, **235**
mushroom
    lamb shank trahanas 98-9, **99**
    mushroom purée 180, **181**
    tuna bowl 190
mustard seed(s), pickled mustard seeds 66-7, **67**

## N

nutmeg 156, 265, 276

## O

oats (jumbo), granola topping 156
octopus 52, 56
    octopus dog 118, **119**
    octopus stifado 82, **83**
okra, chicken okra 104, **105**
olive (Kalamata), Dakos salad 36, **37**
olive oil
    chilli oil 60, 267
    chive oil 38, 40-1, 92, 104, 266
    extra-virgin olive oil parfait 236, **237**
    herb oil 42, 266
    olive oil cream 250-1, **252**
    olive oil flatbreads/tortilla wraps 120, **121**
    olive oil macarons 250-1, **252-3**
olive oil rusks, Dakos salad 36, **37**
onion, confit of pearl onion 146, 184, 271
orzo, beef cheeks giouvetsi 96-7, **97**
ox tongue carpaccio 24, **25**

## P

pancakes 160-2, **161**, **163**
pancetta, Greek eggs Benedict 174
panko breadcrumbs 26, 46, 80
parfait, extra-virgin olive oil parfait 236, **237**
parmesan, tuna parmesan 80, **81**
pasta
    beef cheeks giouvetsi 96-7, **97**
    dolmades 112, **113**
    eel carbonara 76, **77**
    hylopites 76, **77**
    lamb shank trahanas 98-9
    spicy chicken bowl 188, **189**
    stuffed courgettes 40-1, **41**
    trahanas 40-1, **41**, 98-9, 112, **113**, 190, **191**
    tuna bowl 190, **191**
pastry 218-59
    chocolate tarts 240-2, **243**
    choux pastry 224-6, **227**
    *see also* filo pastry
pâté brisée 30-1
pavlova, strawberry pavlova 228-30, **229**, **231**
peanut butter
    milk chocolate peanut tarts 241, **243**
    peanut butter & banana Greek toast 165, **167**
    peanut butter chocolate crumble 162, **163**
pearl barley 78, **79**
pepper (Padron)
    eggs saganaki 184
    grilled feta 114
pepper (roasted red)
    chilli oil 267
    red pepper ketchup 273
pesto, basil pesto 80, **81**, 116, 272
picanha, coffee beef picanha 142, **143**
pickles 124
    pickled blackberries 44-5, **45**
    pickled mustard seeds 66-7, **67**
pilaf, spinach rice pilaf 48, **49**
pistachio
    berry topping 157
    chocolate mosaic 254-5
    extra-virgin olive oil parfait 236
pitta flatbread 214, **215**
    open pitta lamb 182, **183**
    red mullet pitta wraps 120, **121**
pork 128
    DIY gyros wraps 132, **133**
    souvlaki 136, **137**

port (red) 96–7, 102–3, 180
potato
   mashed potato 100, **101**
   potato chips 95, **95**
   smoked potato salad 124, **125**
prawns mikrolimano 60, **61**
preserving methods 56
profiteroles, Greek coffee tiramisu profiteroles 222, 224–6, **227**
purées
   garlic purée 270
   mushroom purée 180, **181**

# Q

quince, white chocolate quince tarts 240, 242, **243**

# R

raspberry
   berry topping 157, **158**
   galaktoboureko 244–6
   raspberry pudding 244–6
   rizogalo brûlée 168
   very berry pancake topping 160
red mullet 144
   catch of the day crudo 64, **65**
   red mullet pitta wraps 120, **121**
rhubarb jam 26, **27**
rice
   rizogalo brûlée 168, **169**
   spinach rice pilaf 48, **49**
riganada, tomato riganada 60, **61**, 104, **105**, 126, **127**
rizogalo brûlée 168, **169**
rolls, cinnamon rolls 210–11, **212–13**
rosemary 96–9, 102–3, 266, 271
rye starter 202

# S

saffron 40–1
saganaki, eggs saganaki 184, **185**
salads 32–48
   beetroot salad 44–5, **45**
   Greek salad carpaccio 68, **69**
   Greek salad (*horiatiki*) 34, 36
   smoked potato salad 124, **125**
salmon (smoked), Greek eggs royale 176
salsa
   tomato & coriander salsa 24, **25**, 192, **193**
   tomato basil salsa 116, **117**
salsify chips 96–7

salted caramel sauce 277
   apple crumble Greek toast 165
   milk chocolate peanut tarts 241
   peanut butter chocolate crumble 162
   white chocolate quince tarts 242
salting 56
sauces
   béchamel sauce 95, 102–3, 265
   fricassee sauce 86, **87**
   lemon-oregano sauce 100, 104, 265
   salted caramel sauce 162, 165, 241, 242, 277
   smoked tomato sauce 78, 182, 184, 268
   strawberry sauce 228, **229**
   tartare sauce 138, **139**
   *see also* avgolemono sauce
sea bass
   fish & greens 148, **149**
   kakavia fishermen's soup 74, **75**
   sea bass imam 58, **59**
seafood 50–86
   to share 72–86
semolina 246, 258–9
sesame seed 28, 198–9, 208–9
shallot, confit of shallot 82, 104, 271
sherry caramel vinegar 274
   beetroot salad 44–5
   chicken okra 104
   octopus dog 118
   octopus stifado 82
sides 110–26
simple syrup 165, 224–6, 270, 276
skate wing bottarga 84, **85**
skordalia 44–5, **45**
smoking 56
snacks 110–26
soup
   cherry soup 236, **237**
   garlic soup 70, **71**
   kakavia fishermen's soup 74, **75**
sourdough bread
   eggs saganaki 184
   fava 22
   green kayanas 178
   mountain eggs 180
   skordalia 44–5
   sourdough rye bread 20, 44–5
   taramas 20
   village eggs 172
   village sourdough 202–3, **204–5**
souvlaki 136, **137**
soya caramel 188, 275
spanakopita 30–1, **31**
spice rub 132, **133**, 188, 275
spinach

black-eyed beans 82
   eggs saganaki 184
   spinach rice pilaf 48, **49**
squid 52
   squid matsata 70, **71**
   squid skewer 116, **117**
starters
   levain starter 202–3
   for pitta flatbreads 214
   rye starter 202
stifado, octopus stifado 82, **83**
stocks
   chicken stock 262
   fish stock 263
strawberry
   berry topping 157, **158**
   strawberry pavlova 228–30, **229**, **231**
   strawberry sauce 228, **229**
strawberry jam
   berry topping 157, **158**
   very berry pancake topping 160
sweet treats 248–59
syrups
   ginger syrup 244–6
   honey syrup 210–11, 256
   simple syrup 165, 224–6, 270, 276

# T

Tabasco 24, 116, 178, 192
tahini
   Greek yoghurt with tahini & banana topping 157, **159**
   tahini brioche 138, **139**, 208–9, **209**
taramas 20, **21**
tartare sauce 138, **139**
tarts, chocolate tarts 240–2, **243**
thyme sprigs 64, 66–7, 74, 98–9, 180, 262, 263, 266, 270–1
'tiger' craquelin 202–3
tiramisu, Greek coffee tiramisu profiteroles 222, 224–6, **227**
toast, Greek toast 164–5, **166–7**
tomato
   aubergine imam 122
   avocado mash 178
   Dakos salad 36, **37**
   DIY gyros wraps 132
   fish stock 263
   Greek salad carpaccio 68
   grilled feta 114
   kakavia fishermen's soup 74
   kale & feta bowl 192
   monkfish fricassee 86
   moussakas 95
   red mullet pitta wraps 120
   red pepper ketchup 273

smoked tomato lobster 78, **79**
smoked tomato sauce 268
tomato & coriander salsa 24, **25**, 192, **193**
tomato basil salsa 116, **117**
tomato riganada 60, **61**, 104, **105**, 126, **127**
see also confit of cherry tomato
tomato jam 80, 96–7, 269
tomato sauce (smoked) 78, 182, 184, 268
tonka bean 241, 258–9
tortilla wraps
   DIY gyros wraps 132, **133**
   olive oil tortilla wraps 120, **121**
trahanas, lamb shank trahanas 98–9, **99**
trout/salmon roe
   giouvarlakia dumplings 92
   Greek eggs royale 176
truffle (black)
   lamb shank trahanas 98–9
   mountain eggs 180
tsoureki 216–17, **217**
tuna
   stuffed courgettes 40–1, **41**
   tuna bowl 190, **191**
   tuna ladolemono 66–7, **67**
   tuna parmesan 80, **81**
turbot, charcoaled turbot 146, **147**
tzatziki 18, **19**, 132

## U

*umami* 56

## V

vanilla
   almond cream 210–11
   baked feta cheesecake 238
   chocolate tarts 240–2
   extra-virgin olive oil parfait 236
   galaktoboureko cream 246
   hazelnut crumble 276
   poached quinces 242
   raspberry pudding 244–6
   rizogalo brûlée 168
   vanilla cream 228, **229**
vasilopita (New Year's cake) 206, **207**
veal liver in caul fat 140, **141**
vegetables 32–48, 110
vine leaves, dolmades 112, **113**
vinegar *see* sherry caramel vinegar

## W

walnut
   beetroot salad 44–5
   Greek yoghurt with tahini & banana topping 157
   melomakarona 256
   moustokoulouro Alaska & sandwich 232–4
   skordalia 44–5
   vasilopita (New Year's cake) 206
wasabi, Greek yoghurt wasabi 42, **43**
'waste not, use all' philosophy 144
white chocolate
   coffee crumble 225–6, **227**
   olive oil cream 250–1, **252**
   vanilla cream 228
   white chocolate & cheese cream 242
   white chocolate quince tarts 240, 242, **243**
white wine
   beef cheeks giouvetsi 96–7
   chicken stock 262
   lamb shank trahanas 98–9
wraps
   DIY gyros wraps 132, **133**
   red mullet pitta wraps 120, **121**

## Y

yellowtail, Greek salad carpaccio 68, **69**
yoghurt *see* Greek yoghurt

This cookbook is the result of the amalgamation of our childhood memories, our experience of running restaurants serving thousands of international guests, and our passion to build upon our traditions to create modern Greek food.

Writing our first cookbook has been a stressful and lengthy process. It took us many hours of internal negotiations to decide the list of recipes included in this book. Adapting them so that they can be re-created at home without the need for expensive equipment found in restaurants was a challenging task. The days we all spent together at the photo shoot were filled with good vibes, laughter and creativity. From the first day we clicked as a team as we shared the same passion to create a wonderful cookbook. At the last camera click we were all very tired, excited and happy – we had photographed all the dishes, yet at the same time we felt sad that it had come to an end and we would not meet up the following day for another shoot.

We have been blessed to be surrounded with some exceptionally talented people whom we would like to thank.

Our publisher Elizabeth Bond and Penguin Random House for their unconditional support and for believing in this cookbook.

Our editor Heather Thomas for undergoing the mammoth task of reading and correcting all our texts. Believe us, this was not an easy thing to do.

Our book stylist Lucie Stericker for her inspiring creativity, kindness and guidance. A true pleasure to work with.

Our immensely talented photographer and good friend Lateef Okunnu whose skills have given a new perspective to this book.

Last but certainly not least, our entire team who came together to create, prepare, test and cook all these dishes. We are blessed to have you in our lives and to call you our colleagues.

**NIKOS & ANDREAS**

I would like to dedicate my first cookbook to my family!

My children Lefteris and Yria, the love and meaning of my life, my parents who shaped me, my sister who was always there for me, and Vassia, the most kind-hearted and considerate person.

Last, but not least, Andreas, a true friend who believed in me without any hesitation and judgement in the biggest turn I had to take in my life.

**NIKOS**

This epic journey would not have been possible without a few very important people in my life whom I would like to thank:

My mum and dad for giving me the assets to chase my dreams. Thank you!

My entire family for their support throughout these years. Your ongoing moral and financial support when needed is something I am forever grateful for.

My wife Elena, whom I met in this restaurant, and our two wonderful children Lydia and Emmanuel.

And, finally, my friend and partner in crime, Nikos. This journey would not have been possible without you.

**ANDREAS**

Ebury Press, an imprint of Ebury Publishing
Penguin Random House UK
One Embassy Gardens, 8 Viaduct Gdns,
Nine Elms, London SW11 7BW

Ebury Press is part of the Penguin Random House group of companies whose addresses can be found at global.penguinrandomhouse.com

Copyright © Andreas Labridis & Nikos Roussos 2024
Andreas Labridis & Nikos Roussos have asserted their right to be identified as the author(s) of this Work in accordance with the Copyright, Designs and Patents Act 1988

Penguin Random House values and supports copyright. Copyright fuels creativity, encourages diverse voices, promotes freedom of expression and supports a vibrant culture. Thank you for purchasing an authorized edition of this book and for respecting intellectual property laws by not reproducing, scanning or distributing any part of it by any means without permission. You are supporting authors and enabling Penguin Random House to continue to publish books for everyone. No part of this book may be used or reproduced in any manner for the purpose of training artificial intelligence technologies or systems. In accordance with Article 4(3) of the DSM Directive 2019/790, Penguin Random House expressly reserves this work from the text and data mining exception.

First published by Ebury Press in 2024

www.penguin.co.uk

A CIP catalogue record for this book is available from the British Library

ISBN 9781529944136

Publishing Director: Elizabeth Bond
Editor: Heather Thomas
Production: Percie Bridgwater
Design and art direction: Lucie Stericker @studio 7:15
Reprographics: Alta Image London
Photography: Lateef Okunnu

Printed and bound in Germany by Mohn Media GmbH

The authorised representative in the EEA is Penguin Random House Ireland, Morrison Chambers, 32 Nassau Street, Dublin D02 YH68.

Penguin Random House is committed to a sustainable future for our business, our readers and our planet. This book is made from Forest Stewardship Council® certified paper.